HOW TO BORROW
YOU NEED TO BUILD A
GREAT PERSONAL FORTUNE

Herbert   Holtje
and
John Stockwell

PARKER PUBLISHING COMPANY, INC. West Nyack, N.Y.

© 1974 *by*

Parker Publishing Company, Inc.
West Nyack, N.Y.

Reward Edition 1982

Library of Congress Cataloging in Publication Data

Holtje, Herbert.
    How to borrow everything you need to build a great
personal fortune.

    1. Success. 2. Business. 3. Loans. I. Stock-
well, John, joint author. II. Title.
HF5386.H674   650'.12   73-20233

THIS BOOK IS FOR THOSE WHO WANT MORE THAN THE $25,000 A YEAR THAT MOST PEOPLE CALL SUCCESS

This book is going to jolt you. And, it's going to jolt the insiders who thought that their secrets of rapid wealth-building were safe. You will be most surprised to learn that the secrets we are going to give you can be used anywhere—and by anybody.

Over the years, you have no doubt heard of many get-rich-quick schemes. Most require special abilities, talents, equipment, real estate, or money. Others require special connections with important people. What it boils down to is this: If you've got the money, special talent, equipment, and the other things needed, it's simply a matter of going through the motions. There is truth in the old saying: "It takes money to make money."

But what if your sole possession is your drive to build a fortune? What if you have nothing but a paycheck that is used up to cover your weekly expenses? What if you have no important connections—and perhaps even a shaky credit reputation? Then this book is for you!

This just might be the most important day in your life. After all, you have just proven that you do have the drive to build a fortune—you have begun to read this book. And, it is this book that can give you the answers and help you need to build a fortune faster than you ever dreamed.

Before you go any further, we want to warn you that you will need many of the things we have just mentioned. And, we want to warn you that it will take some effort on your part. You will have to work at building your fortune. But—with the time-tested, hidden secrets you will discover in the pages of this book, the work will actually be fun, and you will be able to get everything you need by using a completely new concept we discovered—Total Borrowing.

BORROWING IS THE FOUNDATION OF ALL WEALTH

There is much more to borrowing than the gathering of loaned money. Everyone who builds a fortune must have two other very important assets if he is to succeed. Without these assets, most ventures are doomed to failure. But, with them, you cannot help but gather riches. We have been able to reduce the combination of these three assets to a very simple formula that is explained in detail in Chapter 1. This formula will set the stage for all of your wealth-building activity, and anyone can use it—anywhere, anytime.

HOW YOU CAN HARNESS THE POWER OF TOTAL BORROWING

After the few minutes it takes to read this simple formula, you will be able to cash in on the one secret that lets everyone become a millionaire— *Total Borrowing.* By using the time-tested total-borrowing technique we give you here, you will be able to get anything you want—money, property, buildings, tools, machinery, raw materials, and the one thing that will actually permit you to go into any business you choose without having the special abilities of others who have succeeded in similar ventures. We are going to show you how to use a concept of infinite financial power called *O.P.T.* Like the concept of O.P.M. (Other People's Money) O.P.T. will let you harness the strength, talent, and ability that others have spent their lifetimes building. *Other People's Talent* is yours for the asking—if you know how to ask and how to put it to use in your own personal fortune-building activities. We are going to show you how you can tap the brain power of a college faculty, how you can get bankers, lawyers, accountants, and other highly-paid professionals to help you without a fee. And you will read the story of Warren H., a man with nothing more than an idea in his pocket, who turned total borrowing into an annual income of better than $100,000.

HOW YOU CAN GET AN AAA-1 CREDIT RATING IN 40 DAYS, REGARDLESS OF YOUR PRESENT CREDIT SITUATION

The key to wealth is credit, and without credit, you will be stymied. But, we will reveal to you the insiders' secret of building an AAA-1 credit reputation in 40 days with a method so powerful that you will end up with several bank accounts, as well as the personal friendship of very important credit people. And, you will also have cash in your pocket, and a wallet full of credit cards.

You will read of George T., and how he was able to use our secret to build a solid-gold credit rating—and a fortune—in his own business. We call it the *40 Day Fortune Plan,* but George called it a miracle. When you read about this simple plan you will see why there are so many millionaires in the country today, and why you can be one too.

You will also be treated to the insiders' secret of becoming one of the elite circle of credit buyers in the finest stores. You will use the "CAT," our *C*redit *A*ction *T*echnique. It is the final step in establishing you as a person to be respected and accorded the privileges of the wealthy.

With your newly acquired AAA-1 credit rating, you will be able to:

- Borrow money more easily than others;
- Get money at a moment's notice;
- Eliminate the need to fill out a loan application every time you need money;
- Enjoy the power that goes with being able to lay your hands on $5,000, $10,000 or more at a moment's notice;
- Close big deals;
- Go into businesses easily and quickly.

HOW YOU CAN PROFIT FROM THE EXPERIENCE OF OTHERS

Throughout this book, we will tell you of people who started with very little, and by using our Total Borrowing methods, were able to build great personal fortunes. These people started with nothing but the desire to become rich, and today are wealthy, respected members of the community.

You will learn how you can have your business, product or service appear on television, on radio, and in newspapers and magazines without investing a cent!

You will learn how to get editors of national magazines to give you thousands of dollars worth of publicity for any of your products at no cost.

All of these secrets are told in the stories of people who have "made it." The moment you read their stories, you will be on the same path to success.

HOW YOU CAN ACQUIRE A BUSINESS WITH LITTLE OR NO CASH INVESTMENT

A little-known, but very powerful, method we give you will put you in the driver's seat of a wide variety of businesses, again without having to spend a cent. You won't even have to borrow to do it. It is being done every day, but the people who have been doing it have kept it a closely-guarded secret for years. Now, it's yours to use—to build your own personal fortune.

YOUR WEALTH IS ONLY JUST BEGINNING

Once you build your fortune, you will find that the techniques revealed in this book can be used to actually multiply your fortunes. You will be able to apply the strength of leverage to everything you do to the point that your fortunes will grow without effort on your part—truly an automatic income for life.

You can do all of this—and much more—with Total Borrowing. It makes no difference what level of wealth you want to reach. The success-tested techniques we will describe to you in the pages of this book can be used to build millions or simply a comfortable second-income business. Decide what you want, and then follow the principles we describe and you can achieve whatever goal you set. You can use these methods anywhere. Incredible as it may seem, people have used these methods in remote country areas as well as in the hearts of big cities, all with the same fantastic results.

Resolve now that this book will be your guide to a great

personal fortune. Begin reading it immediately. Read it regularly until you have covered every page. Then, as you begin to apply the principles we disclose, refer to the book for all the little details that will mark you as a person destined to acquire wealth.

YOU HAVE ALREADY TAKEN THE FIRST STEP

In truth, you have just taken the first step in Total Borrowing. You are borrowing knowledge from us, the authors, and from the many successful people whose stories of wealth and independence have made this more than a book—*it is your blueprint for success.*

Herbert Holtje
John Stockwell

CONTENTS

1

DISCOVER THE POWER
OF TOTAL BORROWING

"Neither a borrower nor a lender be."

Too many people take this homily literally, and use it as a guiding principle in their day-to-day life. These are the people who are proud to say that they "owe no man." They like to pay cash for everything they buy. To such people, debt is almost a sin.

We venture to say that you can number quite a few people like this among your acquaintances. But, now ask this crucial question: how many among them are *truly wealthy*? Our guess is that there will be few, if any. Why? The answer is simple.

BORROWING IS THE FOUNDATION OF MOST WEALTH

Suppose everybody believed they should "neither a borrower nor a lender be." Here's what would happen overnight:

- Every bank would have to close its doors
- Every insurance company would go out of business
- Everyone with a mortgage would suddenly discover himself on the street
- Most people driving automobiles would face the un-

pleasant prospect of having to walk instead of being able to drive.

*   All of industry and commerce would grind to a halt

If we truly believed one should "neither a borrower nor a lender be" we would soon find ourselves in the middle of a financial Stone Age. For example, when you put money in the bank, you are actually "lending" your money to the bank. They pay you interest for the use of this money. In turn, banks lend this money to a borrower who pays them a higher interest. You make money . . . the bank makes money . . . and the borrower uses the money productively. Everyone benefits.

When you buy an insurance policy, you are again actually lending money. They, in turn, lend it to people and businesses for the building of hospitals, stores, office buildings, shopping centers, schools, and for the good of all people. They charge interest and these earnings enable the insurance companies to pay you dividends and to settle policy claims.

How many people do you know who have paid all cash for their home or car? Very few, we would guess. How many people would be able to enjoy the comfort and security of living in their own home if they had to wait until they had accumulated the total cash needed to buy a house? And, if they did wait, where would they keep the money safe for all those years if there were no banks?

If credit didn't exist, industry would find it impossible to function. Can you imagine General Motors paying cash for a million dollars worth of steel on delivery? The point is this: "Neither a borrower nor a lender be" no longer makes sense in today's modern economy. It would be both a curse and tragedy for such a situation to come to pass. Every successful business is both a borrower and a lender, and the successful businessman is the one who knows how to take advantage of both these techniques.

BORROWING — YOUR PATHWAY TO PROFIT

What is the first thing that comes to mind when someone mentions the word "borrow"? Most people think of money, and rightly so. In this book, we are going to spend a great deal of time showing you how to borrow money and how to use this money as a powerful springboard to success. But, there is more to borrowing than money. And, for the first time in any book, we will introduce you to the concept of "Total Borrowing."

HOW TO USE TOTAL BORROWING
TO BUILD WEALTH FAST

Early in our research, we discovered that some people move more swiftly down the path to wealth than others. We set out to find out why and uncovered a concept that, for the sake of simplicity, we call Total Borrowing. You can understand and use Total Borrowing if you will look at this simple formula:

Total Borrowing $= C + T + I$

Here's what this formula means:

> *C equals Cash* — the money you can borrow by using the techniques we reveal in this book.

> *T equals Tangible Items* — the property and things belonging to others that you can borrow and put to your own use.

> *I equals Intangible Items* — the time and talents, working space, credit, good-will, and reputations of other people.

Let's explore this concept in more detail, because it is very important and actually is the heart of this book.

Cash needs no explanation. It is money. It can be borrowed just about anywhere, and we will show you how to do it.

Tangible Items are things that you will need to make money. They can be tools, machinery, raw materials, buildings, etc. In fact, anything you can see, feel, and use in business are tangible items and we will show you how to obtain them from others for your own personal use.

Intangible Items are your invisible assets. Even though they are unseen, they are essential to the success of every enterprise. We would include here such things as a credit reputation, customer good-will, such legal rights as sales agreements, options, and contracts, and the time and talents of knowledgeable people.

When you sum up all these items—Cash, Tangible Items, and Intangible Items—you have the power of Total Borrowing.

FINDING THOUSANDS OF LENDERS
WAITING TO HELP YOU

Money is important, but now you can build a great personal fortune by borrowing less money than others have done to accomplish the same thing. Surprisingly enough, there are many people who are more than willing to lend you the things you will need to start yourself on the road to success. When you know who these people are and what they have to offer, you will be surprised at how little actual cash money you will need.

In a later chapter, we will tell you of a man who borrowed very little money, but was able to "borrow" the talents of many professionals working for scores of nationally circulated magazines. The help they gave him was worth many thousands of dollars, yet he never had to repay a penny. Today, he is living in a $100,000 home in the country, and enjoys the kind of life you want to have.

If you find this hard to believe, look at it from this very practical point of view: If you can show some person the added advantages he can enjoy if he agrees to lend you some asset he owns—whether cash, tangible or intangible items—you can usually get the use of this asset. But first you will have to convince him of several things:

1. That you are a person to be trusted and whose word can be believed;

2. That his asset will be safe in your hands. In other words, he can enjoy peace of mind knowing that you are fully responsible;

3. And that you will be able to return this asset after you've finished with it. Usually, the lender will want some reward or consideration for this service he performs. If he lends you money, the consideration is the payment of interest. If he lends you something other than money, he will expect either payment at some later date, a share of the profits, or some other consideration. This is only fair. When you have various assets, you too will be seeking ways of making them

grow and will be looking for the same consideration from others.

The important point is this. if you follow the steps we give you in the pages to follow, you will discover all the techniques that will make people want to do business with you . . . to lend you money . . . to offer you the use of their tangible assets . . . and even impart their hard-earned experience to make sure that your enterprise prospers.

HOW TO BUILD A GOOD-AS-GOLD REPUTATION FAST

The main point of this book is to show you how to borrow everything you will need to build a great personal fortune. Consider just what the word borrowing means. A typical dictionary definition says "to borrow" is to "obtain the temporary use of something on the promise of repayment." Here is the secret of success in borrowing: You can borrow *anything* providing you can convince the lender that it will be returned with *something added*. This definition is elegant in its simplicity. Here's how it works:

—You can borrow vast sums of money, provided you can convince the lender that he will get his money back, with interest for its use.

—You can borrow the use of machinery, if you can show the owner that he will get some return for this service.

—You can borrow the use of business real estate if you can show the owner a greater potential return than he is currently expecting.

—You can borrow the experience and talents of knowledgeable people in every walk of life, if you can show them that it will be to their advantage to help you.

In your quest for all of the above, you will run into all sorts of policies, rules, and regulations that lenders will ask you to observe, but it all boils down to one basic fact—what does the lender think of you? What kind of credit reputation do you have? It's all a matter of trust, and we will outline the positive steps necessary to build this kind of reputation.

DISCOVERING YOUR HIDDEN "MIDAS TOUCH"

There is much more to a credit rating, or a reputation, than the numbers that appear on your paycheck, charge accounts, and bank statement. Credit is also a matter of one person trusting another. Have you ever wondered just why one person can borrow almost anything, and another always gets turned down? Basically, it is because this person has the "Midas Touch" — the ability to believe in and to act favorably to proposals. It often takes a lifetime before people learn just what goes into the making of such a personality, but there are a few secrets that can be learned quickly enough so that you can combine them to build the kind of success you want.

Here they are:

— *Be conscious of other people and what they do.* When you seek to borrow something—money, tools, etc.—there is often a tendency to be so deeply involved in your own project that all you talk about is yourself and your own ideas. True, potential lenders want to hear about you and your project, but don't overdo it. After you have made your important points, turn the conversation to the lender. Talk about things that interest him.

Try to make him think that you feel he is an interesting and important person—without overdoing it. If you show a person you are really interested in him, he will be much more likely to do what you want than if you keep talking about yourself and your plans.

— *Believe that people like you.* This is an easy mental attitude to learn, but you would be surprised just how many people lose out because they feel people don't like them. If you show that you expect people to respond in a friendly manner to you, they will.

But, if you act reserved or suspicious, people often hesitate and will not respond as quickly as you would like them to. Have you ever noticed how the quiet people are often left to be by themselves, while the active, outgoing people attract large groups of friends? When you truly believe that people really like you, it helps you get the things you want.

—*Build up the other person's self-esteem.* It is often easy to spot the things that make other people feel inferior. For example, one business executive we know was concerned about the fact that he had never completed college. Even though he was a very successful man in his field, whenever the conversation turned to college, he would become very ill at ease. He didn't have a thing to apologize for. He was financially successful, a good family man, and a person with the reputation for helping others when they needed it. But, he always felt embarrassed by the fact that he never graduated college.

At a meeting with this man, we took pains, one day, to impress him with the fact that the president of a large company, whom he greatly respected, hadn't even gone through high school. He has since learned that the measure of a man comes in many forms, and that he had nothing to be ashamed of. Capitalize on this fact when you talk to strangers.

—*Admit your own faults.* It is not easy to admit a mistake. Most people are willing to forgive a mistake when it is freely admitted. But, when it is covered up and later disclosed, it can cause untold problems.

We have known several people who have been through bankruptcy more than once and have then gone on to become very wealthy people. They didn't hide this fact. They freely admitted it, and explained what it had taught them. They found people to lend them money because, being smart enough to know what they did wrong, and to admit it, the chances were slim that they would make the same mistake again.

—*Have faith in others.* It's often hard to do, particularly when someone you trusted may have disappointed you. But, don't let a bad experience make you lose faith in others. When you are asking people to help you or lend you money, this can be very important. If you show that you have little faith in others, lenders often get the same feeling about you, and will turn down your request.

—*Try to associate with happy, successful people.* It is hard to be discouraged when you are in the company of truly happy and successful people. When we say successful people, we don't necessarily mean those who have made millions of dollars. We mean people who have accomplished what they set out to do, regardless of what it was. Success is measured by whatever standard each individual sets, and successful people can provide the kind of an environment you need to put you in the right frame of mind. Their energy will rub off on you, and you will pick up their enthusiasm in your own quest for personal success.

Stop! Before you read any further, go back and re-read the last few paragraphs. A positive mental attitude is just as important as money, and by practicing the things we have just outlined, you should have very little trouble finding your own "Midas Touch." Memorize these pointers, and consciously apply them each day in your every activity. If your boss bawls you out, don't carry a grudge. You will infect everybody you meet with your hostility. Realize that, whether he was right or wrong, carrying a grudge just puts you at half power. And half power never gets you anywhere very fast.

HOW TO MAKE IMPORTANT PEOPLE ANXIOUS TO HELP YOU

Why do people help people? There are many reasons, and here are only a few:

—because they like you

—because they hope to gain something from helping you

—because they owe you a favor

—because you belong to the same club

—because someone else has spoken for you

You can use some or all of these reasons when you seek the money and assistance of others. Who could refuse to help a person he really liked, or was absolutely convinced was both trustworthy and able to repay the favor in the future.

Obviously, many people—and businesses—are anxious to help because they feel that they would have something to gain. A bank lends you money because it hopes to make money on the transaction. Many people keep a careful mental record of favors, and will not hesitate to call for one in return. Lodge members seldom turn down a brother's request for help, and it is a rare person, indeed, who will not help a person when a friend has spoken for him.

When a corporation wants to float a stock issue, the first person called in after they have talked with their underwriter is their public relations director. He's briefed on the need for the money and the underwriters' approach, and then he goes to work to get a good "press" for his company. This means that he starts to write and place stories in the newspapers and magazines about his company, its products, services, and accomplishments. Never is a word mentioned about the forthcoming stock issue. He carefully builds up a solid image of the company until the point comes where the underwriter is ready to begin selling the stock. At this point, he has stirred up enough interest so that the stock offering seems to be almost accidental— at least in the eyes of the people who buy the stock.

You may not own a big corporation, or even a small business, but you can use similar techniques to insure that you get a good press. Your reputation will get people anxious to help you. And, what's more, you won't need the services of a high-powered, expensive public relations man. You can do it yourself.

HOW YOU CAN GET A MILLION DOLLARS WORTH OF PUBLICITY — FREE

Once you have your business ideas firmed up enough so you can talk about them in some detail, get hold of the editor of your local newspaper. Tell him what you are planning. Tell him that you would like him to run a story about your ideas so that you can attract some possible investors. Even if your idea is not unique, you can give the plan an original twist so that it will attract the interest of readers and possible investors.

Robert L. installed a small printing press, plate maker, paper holder, and cutter into the van of a truck. He brought his "print shop on wheels" to his customers, and the idea was original enough to attract the help he needed to turn this modest operation into a huge, multi-press operation. Today, his combined mobile and in-plant printing company grosses more than a million dollars a year.

Cal T. wanted to start a pet store—a relatively common type of business. His original hook was this: He planned to include a fish-boarding service with his store. People with tropical fish in large tanks often find it difficult to go on a vacation. His fish-sitting idea was unusual enough to get several influential people interested enough to lend him the money he needed to start what is now a very successful business. He now operates several successful pet stores and personally earns over $50,000 a year.

The point is this: people who are potential investors are always attracted by the new, the novel, and the unusual. Call it the gambling instinct, but people are always on the alert to the one-in-a-million opportunity that will multiply their money many times. Keep this fact in mind when you make any business proposal— to a banker, a friend, or a hard-nosed investor.

CHECKLIST OF TOTAL BORROWING TECHNIQUES

As you can see, the old idea of "neither a borrower nor a lender be" is completely out of step with today's economy. If you are going to make it big, you will have to borrow somewhere along the line. You may have to borrow money. You may have to borrow tangible items. You may have to borrow intangible items. But, *you will have to borrow.* Here is a simple checklist to discover your power of Total Borrowing:

- —Borrowing is the foundation of most wealth. Accept this fact and be prepared to use it to your advantage.
- —You can build bigger profits when you know how to borrow correctly.
- —"Total Borrowing" is Cash + Tangible Items + Intangible Items.
- —There are thousands of lenders willing to help you.
- —You do have a hidden "Midas Touch" if you will work at developing it.

2

HOW TO BORROW YOUR WAY
TO AN AAA-1 CREDIT RATING

Throughout this book we will be telling you ways to acquire wealth and the power it brings. When we say "wealth" what is the first thing that comes to your mind? Think hard and what do you see . . .

- a stack of crisp $100 bills?
- a bankbook with entries running into high figures?
- a bulging portfolio of blue-chip stocks and bonds?
- a secret Swiss bank account?

SOMETHING BETTER THAN MONEY

The few examples above represent most people's idea of wealth. Yet, *real wealth* is actually none of these. Consider this for a moment: How much money do you think a typical millionaire carries about in his pocket during his daily money-making activities?

Chances are, many times he has to borrow a dollar from his secretary to tip the man shining his shoes in his office. Yet, that man can walk into the best stores, restaurants, banks, country clubs, or airports and get the best attention in the world. People will flock to his side to cater to his every wish, and provide him with personal service that others must envy. *And he won't spend a penny in cash.*

His secret: *credit*. Everyone this man deals with knows his word can be backed with cash at any time. Things that most people can never afford are thrust at this man with nothing more than a touch of his hand to a piece of paper. *His signature is gold*! Must you be a millionaire to enjoy the benefits and pleasures that such an AAA-1 credit reputation can bring you? Absolutely not!

You can have a wealthy man's credit reputation in as little as 30 to 45 days. You won't spend a cent acquiring this incredibly valuable asset. At the end of this time you will wind up with:

- a solid AAA-1 credit reputation;
- cash in your pocket;
- a string of credit cards in your wallet;
- and a half-dozen bank accounts.

In this chapter we will show you how others have accomplished this feat and how you can follow their methods.

EXPLODING THE GOOD CREDIT MYTH

Most people will tell you that a credit reputation is built slowly over the years by frugal living, by paying bills on the spot, and by never going into debt. The story of Nils J. will quickly prove to you how wrong this idea can be.

Nils learned the trade of carpenter from his father. Later, when he left home, he got a job with a small contractor who quickly recognized the skill that Nils brought to every job. Yet, Nils always dreamed of going into the building business for himself and making it big.

He wasn't letting any opportunities go by. During off days, he would take on small carpentry jobs that contractors disliked to handle. And, when he bought supplies, he would shop several lumber yards for the best prices. He felt morally obligated to pay cash on the spot. His father taught him that he should never owe anyone a cent if he could help it.

PREPARING YOURSELF FOR OPPORTUNITY

A neighbor, impressed with Nil's honesty and skill, asked him one day if he would be interested in building him a brand-new $55,000 home. Nils jumped at the chance to quit working for someone else and to become a contractor in his own right— *his own boss*.

Unfortunately, Nils' dream was quickly shattered when the mortgage company refused to grant a construction loan to start the house. Their reason: to them Nils appeared perfectly capable and honest, but they had no credit rating on him. No credit agency had a file on him, no record appeared anywhere which would demonstrate to the mortgage company that Nils had once borrowed money and proved he was trustworthy by paying it back. You simply don't build a credit reputation when you pay all your bills in cash.

Why was the door of opportunity temporarily closed to this hard-working and honest man? Simply because in today's society credit is more powerful than cash. And, if you want this power, you must understand how to get and use credit.

Credit is the key to building personal wealth. Nils learned this the hard way. But, fortunately, he learned it in time. He was able to get the credit he needed to build the house, and *he was able to do it in only 40 days*. Incredible as it might seem, Nils was able to go from a sorry credit picture to one that was respected by everyone. And, he went on to build a fortune in the building business.

The powerful technique that Nils used has been a well-guarded secret—but we will reveal it so you, too, can build the fortune you deserve. The story we are about to tell you clearly illustrates how this is possible, and just how simple it is for anyone to use.

BORROWING YOUR WAY TO A GREAT CREDIT RATING

We first discovered the technique by talking to George T. George was as ambitious as the next fellow to get ahead. George's failing was that he was a little too enthusiastic about deals that came along, and many times he went ahead without getting all the facts.

As you can guess, in fairly short time George found himself with a stack of bills and obligations he could not meet; his car was repossessed, and he had to sell his comfortable home and move into a cramped apartment in a poorer part of town.

A year had to go by before he got all his affairs untangled: financial statements, court hearings, creditor meetings, the whole works. It was a very unpleasant affair since it left him with absolutely nothing. To make things worse, he lost his job and finally packed up and moved to his wife's parents home.

Then and there, in the depths of his financial crisis, he decided on a course of action that in very short time had him:

- living in a new home in a "wealthy neighborhood";
- driving a brand-new car;
- entertaining new friends without his previous concerns about bills;
- running a business of his own that was growing month by month.

How did George do all this? His first step was to rebuild his credit reputation as quickly as possible. He did it by borrowing his way to an AAA-1 credit rating in his new community.

YOUR FIRST FEW HUNDRED DOLLARS ... AND HOW TO GET THEM

When we tell people of the following method of borrowing their way to a great credit reputation, they are all ears until we tell them that it requires several hundred dollars to get started. Immediately, the scoffing begins.

"If I could lay my hands on four or five hundred dollars, I wouldn't need your advice," they say.

Our reply to comments such as this is, "How much money could you raise if someone showed you how to buy genuine $1 bills for 50 cents each?"

All of a sudden, every scoffer finds it possible to raise $300, $400, $500 or more. In order to take advantage of this fairy-tale bargain, these people said they would be willing to:

- borrow money from relatives
- borrow money from friends
- borrow on their life-insurance policies

- dip into emergency, "rainy-day" savings
- take a second mortgage on their home
- pawn some treasured possession
- cash in their savings bonds
- borrow against pension or profit-sharing funds
- moonlight on a second job
- start a spare-time business*

Obviously, if such a miraculous bargain were to appear, it would be a rare person, indeed, who would not find some way to take advantage of it. In George's case, he swallowed his pride and asked his wife's mother for the few hundred dollars that ultimately made him a wealthy man.

ASK YOURSELF THE IMPORTANT MONEY QUESTION

Take a moment right now and answer this question for yourself: "How would I raise $500 if such an opportunity were offered to me?"

This opportunity *is yours*, and we are sure you will find a way from among the many ways previously suggested. In fact, the *riskiest thing you will do with this money will be to put it in the bank*! Under these circumstances, what more assurance do you need to do everything possible to take this first step into a future of riches?

SHOPPING FOR YOUR FIRST BANK

We will assume a starting point of $500. You can do it for less, and it certainly wouldn't hurt to have more, but $500 is a good start. We want you to put that $500 in the bank, so you should start shopping for savings banks in your town.

Try to pick a bank that gives a premium for starting a new account. For a starter account of $500, you can usually get a fairly nice gift—a toaster, clock radio, or something similar. You might as well get used to these little luxuries while you are on your way to wealth.

---

*There are numerous spare-time businesses that can be started with zero investment In our previous book, *100 Ways to Make Money in Your Spare Time, Starting With Less Than $100*, a number of such businesses are described in detail. The book may be obtained from the Parker Publishing Company, Inc., West Nyack, N.Y. 10994.

Make sure that you open a regular savings account with the full $500. As anxious as you must be to continue your credit-building program, you'll have to wait a few days until your account is posted on all the bank's records.

HOW TO OPEN AN ACCOUNT AND BORROW YOUR LIMIT A FEW DAYS LATER

Now that you have completed this basic step, it will be possible for you to borrow money *without any credit investigation at all*. You can borrow, up to the limit of your recent deposit, simply by using your bankbook as collateral.

At this point you're surely asking, "What kind of sense does this make? All you're doing is putting money in the bank and then borrowing it right back."

This strategic step makes all the sense in the world when you understand the workings of the bank's credit machinery—a money-power machine that can give you everything it gave George T. Borrowing your own money starts a credit chain reaction that puts you on the road to a new credit reputation.

USING THE 40-DAY FORTUNE PLAN

Three days after you have opened your $500 savings account at the first bank, simply walk up to the bank's loan officer and tell him that you want a $500 loan. When you tell him that you will use your personal passbook as collateral, his face will light up and you'll breeze through the loan application. Because this is a risk-free loan for the bank, they will not check further into your credit.

You now have a bank account for $500 that is drawing interest and $500 in your hand. Because you have used your bank book for collateral, it is "frozen" and you cannot draw it out, but it is still actually earning you interest.

Take this $500 and head to the next bank on your list. Be sure it is one that gives you a decent gift for a new account. Deposit the $500. Three days later, make a visit to the loan officer of this bank and arrange for a $500 loan against your passbook.

Repeat this performance at three more banks until you have five bank accounts, each for $500 on deposit, and each drawing interest. You also have a $500 loan at each one of these banks, secured by the passbooks. And, most important you still have your $500—*cash in hand*.

Don't be misled into thinking that we are showing you how to manufacture assets out of thin air. Even though you have five bank accounts totaling $2,500, you also have five bank loans totaling $2,500. One washes out the other. *But, be sure to keep firmly in mind the purpose of this chain of activity—to build an AAA-1 credit rating!*

BUILDING CREDIT WITH YOUR PERSONAL CHECKING ACCOUNT

Now, take your $500 cash and go to a sixth bank and immediately open a personal checking account. Your credit-building chain reaction was started when you opened your first savings account and you are now about to take the most important step in the whole process. You will soon begin methodically to pay off each of the loans with your own personal checks, using the $500 you deposited in your new checking account.

Appreciative bankers keep an eye on people who make regular payments on loans, and this is just what you are going to do In fact, you will make early payments, long before they are ever due. This immediately identifies you as a conscientious bill payer, and someone who can be trusted. And, after all, credit is nothing more than a matter of trust.

EVERY PAYMENT IS A CREDIT BUILDING BLOCK

Three days after you have opened your checking account, sit down and start writing some checks. This kind of check writing will be a very pleasant experience, because you will be building a wealthy man's credit rating with each check you sign. Draw checks for the amount of payments due on each of the five loans, and take them to the banks. You will be paying the first month's installment almost a month in advance. Imagine the look on the banker's face when he sees your early payment check arrive.

Wait one full week. Then, write checks for the second payment on each of the loans. You will be paying the second installment almost two months in advance. If you thought your banker was happy to see your first early check, you can imagine his delight when your second payment arrives.

Wait another full week, and then repeat the performance again.

Here's where you stand with the banks:

- you have five savings accounts, each for $500;
- you have five bank loans outstanding, each for $500;
- you have a very active checking account;
- you have made regular payments on each of your loans;
- you are *three months ahead* on the payments of all your loans;
- and the whole process took only 40 days from the time you opened your first bank account.

NOW LOOK AT YOUR CREDIT RATING!

Regardless of any previous credit rating, once you have made the three early payments, each bank will automatically give you an AAA-1 credit rating for future loans at the bank or to credit bureaus seeking information on your credit standing.

If you have ever filled out a credit application to buy furniture, a car, or any other big ticket item, you know that the application blank seldom asks for more than three credit references. If need be, you can now give five banks as credit references, all of which will be only too happy to substantiate your AAA-1 credit rating with them. And, after all, the bank is the best possible reference you could have.

Here are just a few of the doors you can open with your newly-found credit. You can:

- open charge accounts at the best shops in town;
- stuff your wallet with credit cards;
- apply for big personal loans on your signature alone;
- apply for a mortgage;
- buy a car;
- take vacations now and pay later;
- enjoy the status that comes with unquestioned credit.

You can shorten the process to 30 days if you open savings accounts at three banks and stop there. We suggest five banks because the extra accounts will come in handy when you want to build further on your AAA-1 credit reputation. This process will be described in the next chapter.

USING THE WEALTHY MAN'S CREDIT RATING

Ask any man on the street, and he will tell you that you can't get something for nothing. But, you have just gotten the most valuable asset in the world for next to nothing. How much has your new-found credit rating really cost you? Figure it out.

Interest rates vary from state to state and time to time but here is essentially how it will work out for you:

- Your five saving accounts will be *earning* you maximum interest.
- Your five loans will be *charged* minimum interest rates because they are secured by the best collateral in the world, your own savings account.
- Your checking account charges shouldn't run more than a dollar or two per month.

While it is true that the interest that you will pay for the loans will exceed that which the bank pays you, if you shopped carefully for banks that offered valuable premiums for new accounts, you will have earned a big plus. In the worst of cases you might be out $20 to $30. Certainly a small enough price to pay for an AAA-1 credit reputation.

HOW TO WIPE OUT YOUR DEBTS
AND LEAVE YOUR CREDIT INTACT

You may ask just how $500 in your checking account can be used to pay off the $2500 in loans that you now have. The answer is quite simple. As you begin to pay off these loans with the available $500 in your checking account, each payment "unfreezes" an equal amount in your savings account that was used as collateral for the loan. After you have made the first few payments we suggested, you will have unfrozen enough money so that you will be able to withdraw the next month's loan payment. As you withdraw each monthly payment from the unfrozen amount, place it in your checking account and use personal checks to make the next payments. An active checking account is also a sign of healthy credit.

While it is possible to close out each of these accounts as we have described, we suggest that you leave a few dollars in each account, and use other personal money to complete the loan payments. It is most wise to have these accounts remain active to keep the banker on your side.

HOW TO OPEN CHARGE ACCOUNTS
AT THE BEST SHOPS IN TOWN

Now that you have laid a solid foundation with the banks, start cashing in on your efforts by opening charge accounts in the best stores in town. It is simply a matter of asking for and filling out a standard form. On the bottom, they will ask for three credit references. You can proudly list three of the most solid banks in town. A few days later you will get a charge plate together with a personal letter from the credit manager welcoming you to their family of preferred customers.

You may have one or two favorite stores in which you prefer to shop, but you should strive to make one or two small purchases in all of the stores in which you now have a charge card. Here's what this will do for you:

- you will keep your accounts on active status;
- you will usually be informed of price-cutting sales before they are advertised in the local papers;
- you will be taking positive steps toward building and maintaining your credit reputation.

NATIONWIDE CREDIT IS NOW YOURS

Now that you have a fine credit reputation in your home town, it is time to expand it to all 50 states of the U.S.A. You do this by applying for all of the nationally honored credit cards including:

- gasoline cards
- auto rental cards
- air travel cards
- national cards such as Master Charge and Bank Americard
- hotel cards
- national chain stores

Credit applications for all of these cards are readily available. Whenever you see one, pick it up, fill it out using your banks as references, and send them in. You will get your cards as fast as the computers can process them. A word to the wise: be patient and do not mail all of these applications on the same day. Because many of these companies will be using the same credit bureau for checking, you do not want all of your applications to appear at once. While there is nothing illegal in what you are doing, it often delays processings for cards by raising unnecessary questions. You can mail one or two a week and be reasonably sure that they will breeze through.

HOW TO TRAVEL WITHOUT CASH

By now you have worked very hard to set off this carefully planned credit-building chain reaction. If you followed our advice, you now have half a dozen bank accounts, including a very active personal checking account. You should have a dozen credit cards in your wallet that should give you unquestioned credit anywhere in the United States. Think about this for a moment. Isn't this what a millionaire's life is really like? You can travel, stay at the best hotels, and shop at the finest stores without using a penny of cash.

It is probably time for a vacation. You owe it to yourself and we urge you to take it.

HOW TO USE THE CREDIT ACTION TECHNIQUE TO EXPAND YOUR CREDIT

Now that you have an impeccable credit rating, and a pocket full of credit cards, it's time to go one giant step further. Our Credit Action Technique—CAT—will put you among the most elite of credit buyers. These are respected customers whose monthly transactions amount to hundreds of dollars in each of the stores in which they have credit accounts.

In order to appreciate this technique, you should understand the billing procedure used in many stores. Each time you make a credit purchase, here's what happens:

- your credit account is charged for the amount of the purchase;

- when full payment is made, your account is cleared, showing a zero balance.

If you will look at some of your store bills, you will notice that "credits" and "payments" are usually combined in one column. What this means is this:

- whether you pay your bill, *or return the merchandise*, this column shows the transaction as having cleared your account;
- this means that you can buy merchandise, return it promptly, not make any payments, and still give the impression of being an active, respected customer with no bills outstanding.

HARNESSING THE CREDIT ACTION TECHNIQUE

To take full advantage of the Credit Action Technique, start using your credit cards immediately. Make purchases in several stores of nonpersonal items that can be easily returned for full refund. Take your purchase home, wait a few days, then return your purchase to the store for your full credit. Remember, you will not get a refund because you haven't paid for the purchase. Your account will simply be credited in the credits and payments column we just mentioned. To most credit managers, your record would appear to be active and running into substantial amounts each month.

Again, you might ask, "Just what is the purpose of all this activity?" We repeat, the whole purpose of this transaction is to continue the chain reaction of credit events that are programmed to build your AAA-1 credit reputation. But, remember this, some stores keep records of returns, and they will discover that you are not truly purchasing large amounts of merchandise from them. However, this does not effect your credit reputation, and this fact cannot be used to deny you credit at any other store. The reason is very simple: you do not owe any money, and neither are you late with any payments, or holding merchandise long after it is billed to you.

HOW TO FIND OUT WHAT LENDERS THINK OF YOU

A wonderful Federal law now makes it a legal obligation for the lender to tell you, the borrower, or the credit applicant why his application has been denied. Called the Fair Credit Reporting Act, this law now lets you do something about any possible credit refusal, a turn-down on insurance, or even being passed by for a job. This law says that whoever turns you down must give you the name of the credit agency that gave you the poor rating. Here's the nub of this law:

- The credit agency must let you see its complete file on you so that you can determine exactly why you were refused a loan. Should you find any inaccurate information, or data that cannot be verified, they must delete it immediately.

- Any information that you dispute must be checked again by the reporting agency.

- You can enter in your file any explanatory note about any entries you feel are misleading. If, for example, you have been given a bad credit rating by a store that delivered broken merchandise and for which you refused to pay, this can be explained away with a simple note.

- Anyone who uses false pretenses to get credit information on you is subject to a fine of up to $5000, a year in jail, or possibly both.

CHECKLIST FOR BUILDING AND MAINTAINING AN AAA-1 CREDIT RATING

Here is the seven step method for firmly establishing your credit:

1. Keep accounts at more than one bank.

2. Avoid paying cash: have most everything billed to you, then pay by personal check.

3. Use credit cards for all your purchases "on the road" —gasoline, lodging, meals, and entertainment.

4. If credit is refused, or if a dollar limit is imposed, ask for the reasons immediately.

5. Use all your legal rights in making sure a credit bureau has only accurate and up-to-date information on you.

6. Don't be afraid to buy and then return merchandise for credit. This cost is already built into the price of the article; besides, an active account means that you are making full use of CAT—Credit Action Technique.

7. Don't be afraid to borrow in order to get ahead. Every big business depends heavily on borrowed capital.

3

CASH IN ON YOUR
NEWLY-FOUND CREDIT

Believe it or not, you are now sitting on your own barrel full of money. And, we have just given you the tool to tap it. That tool is simply this—credit! And, when you use this tool, you will:

- command the respect and trust of the important bankers in your town;
- get the red-carpet treatment at the best shops;
- travel by first-class jet in the company of the wealthy;
- enjoy the attention, entertainment, and spectacular meals waiting for you in the best restaurants all across the country.

Obviously, you now have in your possession a rich man's credit. Now, we will show you how to turn your AAA-1 credit into cash *at will!*

HOW TO BECOME A MODERN MIDAS

Surely, you recall the fable of King Midas, whose mere touch turned everything into gold. You can be a modern Midas simply by touching your pen to paper. Through the magic of your newly acquired credit, you can now unleash vast sums of money—and this is money that you can use for *any* purpose. And, the sky's the limit as you can see from this true story of Tom O.

Tom was an ambitious salesman who had dropped out of college because he wanted to see some real money action. Selling recreational equipment, he was soon at the $400 a week level, and he had not yet turned 21. But, like most people who are motivated to build a fortune, he simply was not satisfied with this impressive wage. Tom knew that there was really big money to be made, and what's more, Tom knew he'd never make it by working for someone else.

Tom spent a few hours a week reading up on the basics of the mortgage business. With a small amount of actual cash and loads of enthusiasm, Tom so impressed a large insurance company that they loaned him $1,300,000 to build a shopping center in a growing Southern suburb. In pulling this off he actually put up very little money of his own: he succeeded primarily because of his winning enthusiasm.

The shopping center took off, and so did Tom's fortunes. His own mortgage company now places more than $200,000,000 a year in real estate and investment money.

We have told you this true story to assure you that the big leagues are not closed to rookies. Anybody can play—and anybody can win. And, the techniques we are showing you, on every page of this book, are the same secrets we have watched others use to amass large personal fortunes.

WHY YOU CAN NOW BORROW MORE MONEY MORE EASILY THAN OTHERS

To most people looking for money, a banker is a terrifying ogre who sits behind a big desk, asks a lot of embarrassing questions, and then delights in saying "No" to the person humbled before him.

Nothing could be further from the truth!

Remember this simple fact: a banker is simply a merchant just like any other storekeeper. While the other merchants sell you bread, gasoline, clothes, and other tangible things, the banker is in the business of "selling" you money for his livelihood. You "pay" for the money with interest—it's that simple.

You're not afraid of the other merchants, so why should you be afraid of the banker? With your AAA-1 credit rating, any banker will be anxious to cultivate your friendship and sell you his money.

When we explained this simple truth to George T., the man you met in the last chapter, he found it remarkably easy to borrow all the money he needed. He faced his banker with the confidence of a wealthy man, turned his credit to cash, and used that cash to build wealth and security.

On the basis of your newly-found credit reputation, any bank will be delighted to grant you a personal loan. But, a personal loan is just that—"personal." The bank insists that these loans be used for such things as:

- consolidation of bills
- medical expenses
- vacation expenses
- tuition expenses
- or any other expenditure for personal purposes.

Tell the banker that you want this money to start a business and he will turn you down flat and immediately refer you to the commercial loan department. Here, you will find that your personal credit doesn't cut much ice. Unless you already are the owner of a going business, you won't be able to get a low-interest business loan. To his dismay, George T. discovered this depressing fact, and his plans for wealth seemed shattered until he was told about our "Instant Money" method.

INSTANT MONEY IS AVAILABLE TO YOU

You can, of course, tell your banker that you want to use your personal credit to secure a loan for personal purposes. After you get the money, there is very little to stop you from changing your mind about how you will use it. Perhaps your home is in need of a coat of paint, or maybe the kids' teeth need braces. After you get your loan, you might just decide to let the house go another year, and have the braces put on at a later date. There is really nothing to prevent you from changing your mind. As long as you make the required payments on your loans, the banks really don't care.

The method we are about to reveal to you completely eliminates the need for any such "play acting" on your part. You can actually face your banker with a perfectly clear conscience and every statement you make will be honest and totally aboveboard. Best of all, you can get all the money you want the instant you need it.

You can now take advantage of any fast-breaking wealth-building business opportunity. When you seek a conventional loan, business and personal, you are forced to confront your banker and submit to a financial cross-examination. Then, it often takes many days for the loan to be approved—if it is approved at all. Meanwhile, many once-in-a-lifetime opportunities can be lost forever because of the slow-moving wheels of conventional finance.

When we told George of our "Instant Money" method, he quickly discovered that he could:

- get the money he needed at a moment's notice;
- eliminate the need to fill out a loan application each time he needed money;
- avoid facing the banker each time he needed money;
- pay relatively low interest rates;
- avoid the need for cosigners or collateral;
- enjoy the power that goes with being able to lay his hands on $5,000, $10,000 or more at a moment's notice.

CLOSING BIG DEALS WITH INSTANT MONEY

Our Instant Money method gives you a ready source of capital anytime you need it. George T., using our method, soon found the hidden power of Instant Money. While searching for a place to live, George came upon an apartment house that was for sale. The $100,000 price was right, and he felt that he could act as his own superintendent temporarily, and handle the few needed repairs himself. The big stumbling block for George was getting the down-payment and meeting those first few mortgage payments. But, he knew that if he could swing the deal, the monthly rents of about $2,000 would be sufficient to pay all his bills and give him a rent-free apartment on top of everything.

If you will recall, George had borrowed a few hundred dollars from his mother-in-law in order to rebuild his shaky credit rating. With his newly-found credit, George used our Instant Money method to get the cash he needed to make the downpayment on his apartment house.

HOW TO RESERVE AN INSTANT FORTUNE FOR YOURSELF

Once you have established your personal credit reputation, most banks will jump at the opportunity to "reserve" money for you in your own name. And, you can draw upon this money at any time. In fact, banks have a name for this magic method: they call it *ready reserve*. Ready reserve is available only to those who, in the eyes of the banker, have an outstanding credit rating. If you have followed our methods in the last chapter, you are, in all probability, now a member of this respected group.

Here's what ready reserve really is:

1. The banks you have dealt with in your credit-building activity will gladly continue to do business with you, permitting you to write checks for any money which you have in the accounts.
2. But—you can now write checks for thousands of dollars more and still not be overdrawn.
3. The bank actually covers your check with the money it has reserved in your name. This amount must be pre-agreed upon when you and your banker set up your ready reserve account.
4. You pay the bank back at a predetermined rate. In most cases, you pay back one-twentieth of your line of credit each month, plus interest of about one percent per month.

George T. happily found that the maximum ready reserve loans available to him at five of the banks he had already dealt with, while borrowing his way to an AAA-1 credit rating, would automatically put him in the apartment house business. Armed with his solid-gold credit rating, plus already existing checking accounts, George simply took advantage of his ready reserve at the banks and got the down-payment on his apartment house. Here are the three simple steps he decided to take. He would:

- visit each bank and pick up a ready reserve loan application for his existing checking accounts;
- ask each banker just how much ready reserve the bank would be willing to grant him;
- fill out each application in all truth and honesty and mail them back to the banks *on the same day*.

This last step is very important. In each application, there is a question about current loans and lines of credit. Because George had filled out and mailed all applications on exactly the same day, he could write "none" with a feeling of true confidence on each application. He had already paid his credit-building loans and added to his bank accounts.

If George had dawdled, taken his time, and mailed in the applications on different days, his plan would not have worked. As soon as one bank granted him a ready reserve account he would not have been able to claim that he had no loans or lines of credit outstanding. But, because he took the time to carefully build his credit reputation with each bank, all five granted him a ready reserve account at the same time—and without question. George kept all these ready reserve accounts untouched for several months, but when the apartment house deal presented itself, he was able to sit down and write five checks right on the spot for the needed cash down-payment.

Remember, George had five ready reserve accounts, none of which was sufficient alone to provide the needed down-payment. But, when added together, he had more than enough. Actually, he had a few hundred dollars more than was needed to close the deal. With this extra money, he made some simple improvements that enabled him to raise the rents, and his income, immediately.

HERE'S WHAT INSTANT MONEY CAN DO FOR YOU

At this point, you may think that George was some sort of financial genius. Actually, he was not, and George would be the first to admit it. But, as George is fond of saying, "If you can keep a baseball or bowling score, you can surely handle the details of building a fortune for yourself with Instant Money." Here's what Instant Money can do for you:

- you can have a "line of credit" at one or more banks;
- you do not have to face an interview when you want to use your "reserved" money;
- you do not have to waste time waiting for a loan approval;
- you can write a check whenever you please;
- nothing commands respect like money, and you will have the respect of even the most hard-nosed business man.

As you can see, the Instant Money method we have described to you can be one of the most powerful tools in your wealth-building kit. But, like all tools, you should realize that it must be used properly in order for you to profit. Be sure to keep these points carefully in mind:

- Your ready reserve loans must be paid back, beginning one month from the date you wrote the check.
- Your payments will usually be one-twentieth of your line of credit, with a term of 20 months. For example, if one of your lines of credit is for $1,000, your monthly payment is $50 plus the interest on the unpaid balance. Generally speaking, the interest on such ready reserve accounts is one percent per month on the unpaid balance. Carrying this example further, if your line of credit is $2,000 on one account, your monthly payment would be $100 plus the interest charges.
- If you take advantage of several of your lines of credit at one time, be very sure that your investment provides an immediate return so that you can make all the payments, and a profit for yourself.

DON'T BE AFRAID OF MONTHLY PAYMENTS

If you have enough faith in your business ideas, do not let a monthly payment frighten you. After all, how difficult is it for you to make the payments on your car? Remember this: when you make the payments on your car, the car is not making any money. The payments are coming out of your weekly paycheck. But, when you make the payments on your wealth-building business loan, you are building toward the future. You don't have to stretch your paycheck to make these payments.

When you select your business and investigate it carefully, you will be able to predict the income you should get from it. In our previous book, *100 Ways to Make Money in Your Spare Time, Starting With Less Than $100*, we give specific details on this procedure. When you know just what to expect from your business, you can obligate yourself for monthly payments far in excess of what you could ordinarily handle on your weekly paycheck.

USING HIGH CASH-FLOW TECHNIQUES
HELP YOU REPAY YOUR LOAN EASILY

Important business executives often talk of "cash flow" when they discuss corporate affairs with stockholders and their board of directors. There is really nothing mysterious about cash flow, and if you understand it, you will never get in trouble selecting the right business to suit your borrowing capacity.

What is cash flow? It is simply the flow of money into your business from sales and the flow of money out of your business as you pay bills and meet other obligations.

Some businesses have a high cash flow. In other words, the instant you start, or buy into such a business, you have money in motion—both coming and going. There are, of course, businesses that have a low cash flow. Either kind of business can be equally profitable, but before you get started, make sure you know the cash-flow situation of your intended investment.

The important thing to remember when you plan to start a business with your Instant Money loan is that you must have a high cash-flow situation. You will need cash coming in right away to make that first monthly payment and to continue to make the payments as they are due. But, if you chose your business wisely, you will have more than enough to make the payments and to have some money stick to your pockets as well. To help you, some checklists of high, medium and low cash-flow businesses follow:

HIGH CASH-FLOW BUSINESSES— MONEY IN LESS THAN A MONTH

Rental properties—houses, apartment houses, stores, etc.
Leasing, repairing, and renting tools
Restaurant or tavern
Bowling alley
Golf driving range
Fast-food operation
Coin-operated laundry
Retail stores—most types
Taxi and other transportation services
TV and radio repair
Billiard parlor
Gas station
Appliance repair center
Carpet cleaning and similar services
Driving school
Motel operation
Camper and trailer park operation

MEDIUM CASH-FLOW BUSINESSES— MONEY IN ONE TO THREE MONTHS

Printing services
Public relation services
Employment agencies
Travel agency
Manufacturer's representative
Letter shop services
Catering services
Research services
Industrial services and supplies
Mail order business
Accounting services
Business supplies

Newspaper clipping service
Interior decoration
Landscape services
Income tax preparation
Business school operation
Messenger and delivery services
Uniform rental and sales
Rack merchandising

SLOW CASH-FLOW BUSINESSES— MONEY IN FOUR MONTHS OR MORE

All types of brokerage services
Publishing
Most custom designed and produced products
Home improvement services
Imprinted specialties
Legal and insurance investigation
Advertising services
Financing and lending
Building contractor
Many types of commission sales
Convention services
Import/export business
Bill collection

Generally speaking, when you invest in any type of property for its growth, be prepared for a low cash flow. This includes buildings (but not rental), land, and items that are expected to increase in value with age. For example, you might invest in stamps, coins, silver ingots, and antiques.

With this list in front of you, you can probably name many other businesses that may have appealed to you and then be able to tell instantly whether they are going to give you the cash flow needed to make a success with your Instant Money.

The important point to keep in mind is this: with your Instant Money, you must be very careful to invest it in a high cash-flow business. If you don't, you might find it a bit "squeaky" if you are depending totally on your Instant Money loans to get it off the ground.

If you will recall, George T. invested in an apartment house. As you can see from the list, this is a high cash-flow business. The money rolls in every month as rent from your tenants. In George's case, the monthly rent was sufficient for him to:

- make the payments on his Instant Money loans;
- meet the regular mortgage payments on his apartment;
- pay his taxes, insurance and utility bills.

Maintenance and repairs were handled by George himself, and he was able to live very comfortably in a rent-free apartment in his very own apartment house.

THE TYPE OF CASH-FLOW BUSINESSES THAT GIVE YOU SECURITY AND INDEPENDENCE

Cora B. was a beautician who spent long and tiring hours working in someone else's shop. But, she had her own ideas on how a beauty shop should be run. One day, while she was on her coffee break at a near-by diner, she overheard that the owner of a competing beauty shop was thinking about retiring and selling the business. Because Cora had taken the time to build her credit reputation and to establish ready reserve accounts in her own name, she was able to snap up the business even before it was officially offered for sale. She used her ready reserve money to put up the down-payment, $8,000, and she made the monthly payments out of the income from this high cash-flow business. Over the years, Cora has expanded her operation and added four skilled beauty operators. Her personal income now exceeds $30,000 and she simply supervises now, leaving the actual work to her employees.

Cora's beauty parlor is an excellent example of a high cash-flow business, and here's why:

- it is a necessary and sought after service;
- it has regular clientele who seldom go to a competitor;
- customers pay cash immediately for the service;
- it is possible to buy your supplies on good credit terms.

In the beginning of your wealth-building climb to success,

you should always consider a high cash-flow business first. Once you have a successful business piling up profits for you, you can then afford the luxury of investing in any other kind of business, high or low cash-flow. In fact, you should seriously consider this as one of the best ways of pyramiding your profits.

CHECKLIST FOR CASHING IN
ON YOUR NEWLY-FOUND CREDIT

1. Keep all the bank accounts you opened, as we described in Chapter 2.

2. With your AAA-1 credit rating, find out just how much ready reserve each bank will allow you.

3. Apply for these ready reserve accounts all on the same day. You can truthfully say that you have no other ready reserve loans at the time of application if you file all at once.

4. Keep your ready reserve at stand-by until you are sure that you have found the business that will make you a fortune. Then use it to produce your instant money.

5. Be sure to pick a high cash-flow business to give immediate income.

6. Make your payments regularly from profits.

7. Pyramid your profits by investing in other businesses.

4

HOW TO GET PERSONAL
LOANS AT LITTLE OR NO COST

No matter how you look at it, money *is* important. The people who say that they would be satisfied with the basics—a steady job and all the ordinary things of life—are simply making excuses. Obviously, you, the reader, are not content with just getting by, or you would not be reading this book. The chances are that you are thinking of starting your own business, or at least getting a wealth-building spare-time venture under way.

DECIDING HOW MUCH MONEY YOU NEED

Talk to any ten people you meet on the street and ask them, "How much money do you want—where do you want to be in ten years?" and the chances are that you will not be able to get a real answer from any of them. Most people are more concerned with today than they are with tomorrow, and they have no firm idea of just what they can truly accomplish, if they put their minds to it. But, it takes money to make money, and in this chapter we are going to show you how to use the personal loan as a well-spring of capital.

USING THE PERSONAL LOAN AS A STARTER
FOR WEALTH BUILDING

If you are looking for money for a business, and you are already in business, you will have very little trouble borrowing it from any bank with a low interest business loan. But, if you are at the beginning stages and are just now gathering everything you need, including money, you will not be able to get such a loan. While there are many ways of getting money for a business venture, other than business loans, the personal loan is one of the quickest ways of laying your hands on ready cash. In the pages that follow, we will show you how to go about getting a personal loan to use for your business venture and how you can get it for little or no cost. But, before we get into these details, it will be helpful for you to know the inside information bankers use when they decide who gets a loan and who doesn't.

THIS BANKERS' CHECKLIST ASSURES YOUR SUCCESS

When the banker sits down with his loan committee and goes over the loan applications of the day, he may use this checklist to separate the good risks from the poor ones. Study this list carefully, and, where possible, make sure that you measure up to many of the requirements. Often you can upgrade your credit picture.

- *Identification.* The bank wants to make sure you are who you say you are. All you really need here is a driver's license, social security card, or a birth certificate.
- *A relatively permanent address.* Banks want to know where they can contact you. If you've moved around a lot lately, perhaps a friend or relative, who has a permanent address, will vouch for you in this matter.
- *Steady work.* Steady work shows the banker that you can be counted on to become a valued customer as you build your fortune.
- *Where you live.* While it is possible to borrow money anywhere, it is often easier to get money from a bank near you.

- *Previous loans.* Naturally, banks are interested in whether you will be able to repay your loan. If you can show a history of loan repayments, you will automatically be in line for the maximum available for personal loans. If you have done as we suggested in Chapter 2, you will have absolutely no trouble on this score. You already have an AAA-1 credit rating at five important banks. Your line of credit has been established and all you have to do is drop in on your friend, the loan officer, and tell him what you will need.

- *Bank accounts.* Again, if you followed our 40-Day Fortune Plan, you will have five savings accounts and one very active checking account. This coupled with all of your other positive assets will put you in great shape for the maximum in personal loans at any bank you choose.

Remember, you don't have to have a top rating in all these categories. It is a rare person, indeed, who will pass muster with flying colors on every point of the banker's checklist. But, as long as you show a strong trend, and can impress the banker with your good intentions, the chances are that you will get the money you need.

GETTING CREDIT WHEN YOU HAVEN'T HAD TIME TO ESTABLISH A REPUTATION

Many people seeking to establish themselves in a wealth-building venture of their own simply have not had the time to establish a good credit rating. Not that they have done anything shady; rather, they simply are not old enough to have experienced the activity necessary to impress the loan officer.

Many people find this hard to believe, but most bankers are really warm human beings, and when they are faced with a young person with ideas, dreams, drive, and a thin credit reputation, they often look the other way and grant the loan. It's sort of like trying to get a job as a beginner, and having the prospective boss tell you to come back when you get some experience. How are you going to get any experience when everyone wants to hire only an experienced person? But, you will find that many banks are quite willing to invest in the future of some young person. After all, they are just as interested in establishing relations with a bright, promising young person who can turn into a valued customer.

USING PERSONAL LOANS AS A STEPPING STONE TO BUSINESS SUCCESS

As we mentioned earlier, it will be just about impossible for you to get a business loan without already having a going business. However, you will find it possible to get a personal loan for just about any good reason *except* business. This may seem silly. But, the banks simply do not look at it this way. They say a personal loan is for personal purposes, and a business loan is for business purposes. And that's that.

With your new credit rating, you can go to any of the banks in which you have established accounts and borrow your limit in personal loans. Then, with the money in your pocket, you may decide: why not start a business? After all, once you have the money, the only thing the bank is concerned about is your paying it back as specified.

THE FASTEST WAY TO A LOW-COST LOAN

What we have just described is a very effective way to get the money you need on a personal loan from any bank, but there are still many other avenues open to you. One of the quickest ways to borrow money also happens to be one of the ways lowest in cost. We will describe the technique by telling you the story of Martin S., a man with an idea, drive, and very little capital.

Martin was employed by a large aircraft company as a detail draftsman, but business was slow and the raise he was counting on just never materialized. In fact, Martin wasn't sure from day to day whether he would be able to keep his job. While working on a design for a sealable wing tank for an airplane, Martin came up with an idea for sealing opened soda and beer cans. Unlike bottles, which can be resealed if not finished, the contents of a metal can must be consumed or thrown away. Martin was on to something, and naturally he wanted it all to himself. But he needed money.

Martin did not have the time to establish a credit rating. But he didn't need very much money either. He felt that with $1,000 he could do the development work, and get a preliminary patent. He did not want to manufacture and market the product himself. He wanted to protect it, then sell it to a big manufacturer who would either pay him a royalty on sales or buy it outright from him.

USING THE TWO-DAY LOAN WITH NO CREDIT CHECK

In addition to the group insurance his company provided, Martin had had the foresight to buy a straight life insurance policy. He had made substantial payments on it over the years, and found that he could get the $1,000 he needed by borrowing on this policy. There are several advantages to this kind of loan:

- You can get the money almost immediately. In Martin's case all it took was a few days.
- There is absolutely no credit check. After all, the money is "in the bank" because it is money that you have paid into your insurance policy.
- It often has a very low interest rate. If you are interested in this kind of a loan, simply get out your policy. You'll find the rate you will pay specified right on the face of the policy. If your policy was in effect before 1939, the chances are that the rate will be six percent. If your policy was in effect after 1939, it should be about five percent.

YOU TELL THE LENDER HOW YOU WILL REPAY YOUR LOAN

It's true! You can tailor an insurance loan to suit your needs exactly. You dictate the terms to whatever method fits your plans. If you want to make monthly payments, you can do so. If you would like to pay it back in one lump sum, feel free to do it. You can pay it semiannually, or just about any way you choose. When you borrow money on your insurance policy, you write the repayment schedule. Whatever you say goes.

HOW TO BORROW MONEY AND KEEP IT AS LONG AS YOU WANT

This is another great feature of the insurance-policy loan. You can have it for as long as you wish. A year, two years, you name it. But, it is important to keep in mind that as each year passes, you will be charged with another round of interest on whatever is left outstanding. But, considering that insurance loans are often quite low in interest compared to those from other sources, this is often a small price to pay.

Another thing to keep in mind is the ultimate reason for insurance—death. Should you die while you have a loan outstanding, the amount of the loan balance will simply be deducted from the face amount of the policy paid to your estate. But, this is seldom near the amount of the policy, and your heirs will still have the benefit of most of your policy when it is most needed. (It is often possible to make up this loss in value by buying a low-cost term insurance policy. Such a policy can be bought for a short period of time with part of the money borrowed on your straight life policy.)

HOW TO GET A FOUR-PERCENT LOAN
WITH NO CREDIT CHECK

If you are one of the many veterans who continued the GI insurance when you returned to civilian life, you have the source of one of the lowest cost loans available in the country today. You can borrow on your insurance policy, as we have described above, with one very important difference: you will only pay a five-percent interest charge. To get the details on this excellent source of fast money, contact the local office of the Veteran's Administration.

Martin S. was one of those fortunate sailors who had converted the insurance the government carried on him while he was in the navy to a policy on which he made payments as a civilian. Getting his $1,000 low cost loan at four-percent interest, Martin was able to do the developmental work needed on his can stopper and is now trying to sell the idea to a big manufacturer for a large sum of money. Judging from what others have made from similar inventions, Martin could possibly multiply his $1,000 by 50.

USING THE NO-COST LOAN

Carl H. had wanted to be in business for himself for many years. He was working for someone else in a small dental laboratory, when the owner had a serious heart attack. Unable to continue the business because of his health, the owner began looking around for a buyer, but there was none to be found. That is, until Carl spoke up.

Carl didn't have the $6,000 needed to buy the business, and he found it very difficult to arrange for a loan from the commercial sources. Both Carl and his boss were in a tight spot. Carl's boss had to leave the business, but he could find no one with the cash to buy it. If the business closed, Carl was out of a job. So, Carl proposed a no-interest loan from his boss to buy the lab. All he needed was $2,000 plus the amount he had in his savings account, $4,000, and he was in business for himself. Carl's boss agreed and they both got what they wanted. It worked out well for Carl's boss because he did not have to pay taxes on the interest he would have gotten from Carl, and, because he raised the sale price slightly, he gained money on which he had to pay lower taxes—capital gains.

This kind of no-interest loan can often be swung when buying a house. People sometimes have to move unexpectedly, for business and other reasons, and must dispose of their homes quickly. If it happens to be a buyers' market, you can often swing such a no-interest loan to get the home you want.

HOW TO GET MORE MONEY AND TIME OUT OF THE SAME LOAN

Suppose you already have a loan, have paid off about half of it, and now find that you would like more money and more time to pay it off? All you have to do is to talk to the lender about extending the loan. You can reduce your payment amounts as much as half by doing this. What you are really doing is adding to the time already allotted to the repayment.

Let's say you have a loan for $1,000 and have paid off about half of it. You now find that you would be more comfortable with a lower payment. Here's what you do:

- Meet with your banker and tell him that you would like to cut your payments in half.
- He will then simply extend the payment period of the loan to twice what it is now.

- You would have been paying about $83 for the six months left in the loan.
- Under the new payment schedule you will be paying only about $42 plus a certain amount of additional interest.
- If you have taken the time to establish a fine credit rating, you will also be able to borrow even more money at this time.
- You will then have an increased amount of money plus an extended period of time in which to repay it.

HOW TO BORROW FROM YOUR CREDIT UNION AT VERY LOW INTEREST

Warren S. worked for a large manufacturer in Chicago. Warren was a go-getter, and wanted to start a week-end business, but needed money to get it off the ground. But Warren faced the same problem that so many others have—he had not taken the time to establish himself as a good credit risk. And, he did not want to wait the 40 days it would take to get a credit rating.

Fortunately, Warren's company had a credit union, and Warren was able to borrow enough money from it to cover the cost of cement work on his sidewalk, $600. Unfortunately, it turned cold early that year in Chicago, and it was impossible to pour cement. Of course, Warren had already gotten the $600 from the credit union for this work so he simply proceeded to put it to use in starting his week-end business of an inspection service for new home buyers.

Here are the advantages of borrowing from a credit union:

- there is never an investigation, as you would have to go through in a bank;
- you can get the money almost immediately;
- interest rates are usually quite low, compared to commercial loans;
- they are often more lenient when it comes to tardy repayment.

Of course, you must belong to the credit union, but most big companies have now started them for their employees.

HOW TO USE THE CREDIT OF OTHERS
TO GET THE MONEY YOU WANT

A personal loan is granted solely on the basis of your signature. You put nothing up as collateral. It is simply your good word that gets you the money.

If you are finding it difficult to get such a loan, it is a simple matter to "borrow" the credit rating of others to get the money you want. All you do is have someone else sign the loan with you. He becomes a cosigner, and lends the prestige of his good credit rating to you while you are in the process of building yourself and your business. And you have all the money you need.

WHERE TO GET THE CREDIT OF OTHERS

A cosigner may be just about anyone—anyone with the credit rating a bank will accept. This could include any relative, except a wife or husband. You will find that many banks will have your spouse sign the loan with you, regardless of the number of other cosigners you have. But his or her signature will be of no help in getting the loan.

You can use relatives as cosigners, but you should realize that they will then know quite a bit about your finances. If this doesn't bother you, your first choice should be a relative.

WHERE TO BUY THE CREDIT OF OTHERS

If you are turned off by the idea of having Uncle Harry in on your financial affairs as a cosigner, it is possible to actually pay someone with a good credit reputation to act as your cosigner. Simply ask your closest friends, and the chances are that you will get several offers. After all, you will be paying a fee for this service. But, be sure to remind your cosigner that as he signs his name, he is also making himself liable for the debt, should you fail to pay it back. There are no hard and fast rules for the payment of a cosigner and there are no regulations that limit what can be paid. But, try to get away with as little as possible, starting with one percent and stopping at no higher than four percent. After all, you will still have to pay the interest on the loan. And, when you add the cosigner's percentage to the interest, you might have a large load to carry if you give him too much.

CHECKLIST FOR GETTING THE MOST OUT OF YOUR PERSONAL LOANS

1. Decide how much you want, set a goal, and stick to it.

2. Make sure that you meet many of the requirements on the bankers' checklist. It is not necessary for you to be perfect—nobody is—but emphasize your strong points.

3. Consider a personal loan as a practical source for business money, but be sure to understand how to get it.

4. Try the credit-union loan.

5. The two-day, no credit-check loan can be of value.

6. Veterans can use the four-percent, no credit-check loan.

7. The no-cost loan can be used, if you play your cards right.

8. Extend your loan period and get more money in the bargain.

9. Friends can be a fine source of money.

10. You can use the credit of others to get the money you need.

5

COLLATERAL LOANS
ANYONE CAN GET

Say "collateral" to the average person and immediately he thinks of a Simon Legree character holding a mortgage over some poor widow's head. This may have been true a hundred years ago, but today collateral loans can be the quickest wealth-producing avenue you can travel. Most of the really big deals you read about in the business and financial pages of your newspaper usually involve some sort of collateral loan arrangement. And, there is no really good reason why *you* can't start putting together big deals such as these yourself.

COLLATERAL LOANS ARE EASY TO GET

To understand why collateral loans are easy to get, you should first make sure you know what collateral is, how it is used, and how to recognize good collateral when you come across it.

By "collateral" we mean anything of value that can be put up as security for a loan. Collateral can be physical property such as a car, house, or boat. Or, it can be an "invisible" contract or a lease that will guarantee a certain amount of money coming in to cover any loan payments. We'll talk about both kinds in this chapter.

BORROWING FAST WITH PHYSICAL COLLATERAL

Physical collateral is a piece of property of some kind. If you put it up as collateral, the lender will loan you an amount of money that represents a fraction of the value of the property.

For example: you want to buy a car that costs $4,000. The dealer says, "You can have the car for only $500 down. The balance of $3,500 can be financed."

What he really is saying is this: after you put $500 down, you can use the $4,000 car as collateral against the $3,500 loan. If you should default on your payments, the lender can take the car back and sell it for enough to cover the loan he made to you. Right away, you can see some of the advantages and limitations of using physical collateral as a means of raising money.

The limitations are:

- you can't borrow more money than your physical property is worth;
- you will only get a fraction of what the property is worth;
- only items that have generally recognized value can be used as collateral. Valuable family items that are priceless to you are probably worthless to a lender as collateral.

Most collateral is something of recognized value (a $4,000 car, a $32,000 home, $17,000 worth of materials and goods in a warehouse, etc.).

The advantages of physical collateral can be summed up as follows:

- you can get a loan quickly, usually as fast as a lender can verify the value of the asset and the fact that you own it;
- you can still use the asset even though it is used as collateral in certain cases (cars, boats, furniture, etc.).

INVISIBLE ASSETS CAN BE WORTH BIG MONEY

Invisible assets usually are represented by a piece of paper of some sort. That paper can be a contract, deed, lease, or other agreement that brings in money to you.

Edward K. was a small manufacturer selling to a number of customers on open account. At any time during the course of a year, his customers may have owed him a total of $40,000 to $60,000. Ed saw a great opportunity to increase his business by buying out a competitor—all he needed was $30,000 cash, and *in a hurry!*

Fortunately, Ed had the best kind of invisible asset—a string of accounts receivable. Any lender knew that even though Ed's customers may owe him a lot of money in total, they would eventually pay. It's like money in the bank. And Ed drew upon it simply by assigning his accounts receivable to the lender. This is recognized business practice and it is done all the time by banks, factors, and other lenders.

HOW TO BORROW AGAINST FUTURE INCOME

This example highlights a very important borrowing technique—that of borrowing against future income. In general, if you have any source of income that is pretty well assured, you can use it as collateral. Here are some examples:

- an inheritance
- an annuity
- a term bank account
- a bond

HOW TO GET THE BEST DEALS ON COLLATERAL LOANS

There are a few rules you should observe when you're shopping for a loan against some collateral. The first one is: don't take the word of the first lender you approach.

Lenders and bankers are human. In many cases, it's impossible to give a precise value to a piece of property. Sometimes a lender will be loaded with real estate mortgages in a certain area. He will be cautious about lending much more in that particular area because he wants to spread his risk. As a result he may turn you down, or offer you so little as to make it not worthwhile for you to consider the loan. The moral: shop around; you'll be surprised at the variations you get.

The second rule is not to let the lender know all the collateral you have before he asks you. If you have a car, a boat, some furniture, and perhaps some stocks and bonds, don't put it all in front of the banker at once. Let's say, in the preceding case, you want to raise $7,000. The car and boat might swing the loan. Tell the banker about the rest and you'll probably have to put them all up as security for the loan. Bankers are human, we repeat, and being human, they also want to minimize their risks as much as possible.

USING COLLATERAL LOANS TO BUILD YOUR WEALTH

How long would it take you to swing a $400,000 apartment house deal? How much money would you need? This is the kind of question that is put to us often by wealth-seekers wanting to make it big. Most people would dismiss the idea at the start, figuring such money is beyond them forever. Hang on!

George T. saw just such an apartment house deal. To settle an estate, the owners wanted fast action and George gave it to them. Here's how he did it with both physical and invisible collateral:

1. The bank was willing to give George an immediate mortgage of $300,000 on the apartment. This represented three-quarters of the value of the property and is about the limit that mortgage bankers will go on such deals.

2. George found a lender willing to give him a second mortgage of $75,000 at a higher interest rate than the bank charged him for the first mortgage. That still left George with $25,000 to raise.

3. Using the Instant Money techniques of the previous chapters, George wrote himself a check for $25,000 and closed the deal.

With nothing more than his AAA-1 credit reputation, George was able to raise enough money to talk serious business to the apartment house owners. Once the deal was made, he could use the apartment house, and the rents it brought in, as both physical and invisible collateral to get the rest of the $375,000 that he needed to swing this deal.

CASHING IN ON YOUR MORTGAGE

If you have lived in your own home for some years and have been paying off a mortgage, you may have a surprising amount of borrowing power at your instant command. Most people in such a position consider themselves "mortgaged to the hilt," but consider the case of Larry L.

Larry bought a $22,000 home about eight years ago in a good neighborhood. He made his monthly payments faithfully and saw his mortgage decrease at a painfully slow rate. At the end of eight years, he still owed $16,000. But, when we showed him what he was really worth, Larry's eyes lighted up and immediately we could see him planning some real estate deals. Here's what we showed him:

1. In eight years, Larry's house has just about doubled in value. He could easily sell it for $45,000. This is not an unusual situation in today's real estate market. Property values have been rising a little over ten percent per year during the past decade on the average.

2. Larry could remortgage his property for about three-quarters of its present value—about $34,000.

3. With the $34,000 cash, Larry could pay off his original $16,000 mortgage and have *$18,000 cash* left over to invest as he pleased.

4. There was a nice investment property that Larry found exciting—a building that had a going retail business on the ground floor and two apartments upstairs. The property could be bought for $90,000, and brought in total rents of $12,000 a year. All Larry needed was a twenty percent down-payment—and he had it in the $18,000 cash we showed as his "invisible asset."

5. The monthly rents from the building paid all the expenses, the mortgage payments, and the extra monthly payments Larry now had on his increased home mortgage. And he still had a profit left over at the end of the year—plus an investment property that was growing at ten percent a year!

When we spoke to Larry recently, he was negotiating his third real estate deal using the "second-mortgage" technique. "And to think," he said to us, "all that time, I had a fantastic asset that was completely invisible until you showed it to me!"

BUILDING WEALTH WITH THE
SECOND MORTGAGE TECHNIQUE

Most people think a mortgage is the most they can possibly borrow on a piece of property. However, this is not so. Almost any type of property can be mortgaged further with a second mortgage. This sounds formidable but it shouldn't frighten you from a very valid wealth-producing technique.

Generally speaking, a primary lending agency—such as a bank—will lend you only a certain fraction of the value of the property you own or are interested in purchasing. As a rough average, figure on about 70 to 80 percent as a conservative estimate of the market value of the property. Where do you get the rest of the cash you need? A second mortgage will many times provide the answer. Another lender, usually an individual, or a firm specializing in such loans, will loan you the difference, or very close to it. Although they charge more interest for their loan because of the risk, a good investment property will easily pay off this extra expense with profit to spare for you. You can find sources of second mortgages through your lawyer or real estate agent, or by scanning the pages of *The Wall Street Journal.*

TURNING A LEASE INTO INSTANT MONEY

A piece of paper representing a lease on a piece of business property can be a surprisingly good piece of collateral—often times enough to swing a deal without much cash of your own. The lease agreement, in itself, becomes Instant Money. This is money you can use either to finance the deal you have in mind, such as buying the property, or using it as collateral to make a deal on another piece of property. Look how you can make it work:

Example 1

There's an empty store that's been unrented for several months. The reason is all too apparent just by looking at the store. It's old, lacking in modern lighting, and by all standards a pretty unattractive store. The owner is discouraged and is ready to sell out at a favorable price. Here's where you come in. With your imagination for making money, *you* can see the possibilities in the store if only it were fixed up properly. You can see the value and you can make that value apparent to a potential tenant. Once you've signed him up to a fairly long lease, you can borrow the money to finance the deal. You turn the lease into Instant Money because you are now going to the bank with an income-producing property as collateral—just about the best collateral in the world.

Example 2

A lease is a contract, and a contract can often be all the collateral you need to set you up in business. Take the case of Sidney M. Sid was making a so-so living as a salesman of office supplies calling on small businessmen day in and day out. He hankered to quit his constant traveling to service accounts that bought small amounts of stationery and supplies from him. He saw himself making big money leasing office machines. But—how could he finance the machines so he could then rent them?

The answer turned out to be incredibly easy: with his contacts in the various offices he visited, Sid quickly found out that a ready market existed for the rental of new office equipment. Sid spelled out a good deal in his lease arrangement, sold a number of contracts, and quickly turned these contracts into the money he needed to purchase the machines. In a relatively short time, the rentals paid for the machines, and Sid was making a profit without "nickel-and-diming" it for the rest of his life.

HOW TO FIND CONTRACTS YOU CAN TURN INTO COLLATERAL

Contracts of one sort or another can be the most lucrative path to wealth. There are several reasons for this:

- A contract is something you can sell without first investing a lot of money. Once you get a contract, you can borrow the money to invest in the business you've just gotten into.
- There is no limit to the number of different contracts you can sell, thereby pyramiding business upon business and income upon income.

Let's return to Sid who started out by leasing office machines. Within a year of starting, Sid was grossing about $25,000 a year. After paying expenses he netted a scant $10,000. Some plodders in the wealth game stop when they reach some small milestone like this—a five figure income. But not Sid.

Sid realized that there were many other services he could contract for in addition to leasing office machines. Best of all, they were the kinds of services his regular office customers would also want. Soon Sid was providing the following services on a contract basis:

- leasing office machines (his first business);
- renting office furniture;
- contracting for regular delivery services (a number of his customers, advertising agencies, needed frequent daily deliveries between their offices and typographers and art studios);
- auto leasing (several of his clients had a number of salesmen constantly on the road in company cars).

In each business that Sid started, he had nothing but a contract from a customer. Using this contract as collateral, he was able to borrow the money he needed to buy the office furniture, delivery vehicles, and automobiles that he needed for these new ventures.

You can bet he was making a lot more than $10,000 per year for himself after starting these businesses!

HOW TO MULTIPLY YOUR COLLATERAL POWER

Let's say you own 100 shares of the ABC Company, and each share of stock is currently trading for $10. That means that you own $1,000 worth of stocks. You can use these stocks as collateral and any banker will take them as collateral for a loan, with no question whatsoever. The amount of money he can loan you is governed by Federal regulations. You can figure on borrowing about 70 percent the value of your stock. At times, this figure has been as low as 50 percent.

How did you acquire that 100 shares originally? By this time, we think we've given quite a few ideas how to raise $1,000 or even $10,000 without too much trouble.

Here's what you do:

STEP 1. Use your 100 shares of stock as collateral and borrow the full 70 percent or $700.

STEP 2. At $10 per share, you can now buy an additional 70 shares with that $700. Buy them.

STEP 3. Use your 70 shares of stock as collateral for another 70 percent loan, or $490.

STEP 4. Keep repeating this procedure until you get down to your last few shares of stock.

Each time you buy, you'll be paying small brokerage fees, and you will find it impossible to buy stocks at precisely the same price each day. But, even if the market is standing still for the stock you've bought, you'll own about *280 shares of stock*—worth about $2,800, and yet you paid only $1,000 for all the shares! You made each of your dollars work almost as hard as three. If you've picked a stock that is enjoying a solid growth, in a couple of months it can increase as much as 50 percent in value. Stocks have been known to double, triple and quadruple in the same time, but we recommend you stay away from highly speculative issues when you're using borrowed money.

If your stock has doubled in value and you decide to sell at that point, your 280 shares are worth $5,200—and you started with a borrowed $1,000. Pay off all the stock loans if you wish and you have a solid profit of over $2,000 even after paying back your original $1,000.

CHECKLIST OF COLLATERAL LOANS

Physical Collateral

Car

Boat

House

Valuable stamps and coins

Jewelry

Cameras or other expensive equipment

Business machines or tools

Business inventory

Specialized business assets including livestock, oil wells, mines, etc.

Invisible Assets

Contracts for services

Assignments of royalties

Stocks and bonds

Insurance policy cash values

Accounts receivable

Warehouse receipts

Rents from apartments or commercial property

Income from contracts for services

Wills, trusts, and other inheritance rights

6

HOW TO
BORROW BY MAIL

In Chapter 4 we talked about how you can use many different kinds of personal loans as sources of money for your wealth-building activity. If you will remember, these loans were made strictly on your signature—no one would ask you for the title to your car, your bank book, or any other type of security. There is still another way to personally borrow money, but we felt that it was important enough to be included in a chapter by itself. It is the technique of borrowing money through the mail.

WALKING TO YOUR MAILBOX FOR AN EASY LOAN

There are several ways to get money by mail, and we will cover each in detail in this chapter. But, before we do, it will be important for you to begin to firm up just what kind of business you are planning to start with your borrowed money. In this planning, there is one point that must *always* be kept in mind:

- If you are going to finance a business with a personal loan, the amount of capital available to you will be somewhat limited, compared to other methods of raising cash, including stock issues, business loans, etc.

For this reason, we strongly suggest that you plan your business carefully around a venture that requires relatively low capital to get moving. This doesn't mean that you will stay with this kind of a business, but it does mean that your initial operation will get you in business to the point where you can then cash in on low-cost business loans when money is needed. The story of Charles G. will help make this very clear.

Charles was a man with ideas. He worked for a company that manufactured tools. While Charles had no formal education beyond high school, he was the kind of a person who grasped and understood technical and business concepts quickly. As a result, he was quickly promoted within the company's engineering and manufacturing departments to the point where his ideas became the lifeblood of his employer's new products. Charles realized this and yearned to go into business for himself, but he was unable to save enough money from his weekly paycheck to do what he wanted—manufacture tools.

THE MAIL BRINGS MONEY

Charles had decided that he would have to take an intermediate step before he would ever be able to go into the manufacturing business himself. With his knowledge of tools, he decided to become an independent sales agent, a manufacturers' representative, for the company that now employed him and for several other companies with similar products. Here is the key point:

- A business such as this requires nothing but time on the part of the business man. He needs no machines, no stock, and no heavy overhead. He makes his money as he sells his clients' products, and most of them already had customers in his territory that paid him immediate commissions. But, Charles did need money to cover himself until the commissions started rolling in.

He decided to borrow the sum of $14,000 by mail. He then took the following steps:

1. While still working for the long-time employer, he contacted one of the many loan-by-mail sources that advertise in the leading business magazines.

2. He received their forms and filled them out honestly.
3. He mailed the forms back.
4. He collected the money he needed in less than two weeks.

You see, these loan-by-mail companies are designed for just such loans. If you have been working regularly and can meet other minimum requirements, the loan will be granted immediately. Here are the features of such a loan:

- *Complete privacy.* All transactions are handled through the mail. No one ever comes and rings your doorbell, or phones to ask embarrassing questions.
- *There are never any personal interviews.*
- *The lenders never contact your friends,* neighbors, relatives, or business associates.
- *The mail correspondence always appears to be a personal letter.* The envelope never screams out at the mailman, "Mr. Smith is dealing with a lending company!"
- *In some cases the check appears to be written by a personal friend,* rather than a loan company.
- *Loans are granted quickly.* Most of the companies will mail you a check the day your loan is approved.

Charles G. qualified for the maximum this particular company would grant—$14,000. With this money, he was able to pay himself a modest salary, cover his travel expenses, and get his sales agency off the ground. Once this was rolling, Charles continued to pursue his original intention—to start a tool-manufacturing business, similar to that owned by his previous employer. Now, when he needs capital, he is able to go to any bank and take advantage of the low-cost business loan.

HOW LOANS BY MAIL GIVE YOU A FAST START

There are many companies that will lend money by mail, and most of them are competitive when it comes to interest. One of the companies actually advertises that the lender can save as much as 18 percent on interest rates, when compared with other services including banks. What this means is that these people are very interested in getting your business, and are competing with each other for the privilege of lending you money. Let's look at some actual figures taken directly from the mailing piece of one of the prominent mail-order lenders. We will use $4,000 as a convenient example and show you exactly what you pay in finance charges and monthly payments for four different loan periods.

Time Period	Amount Financed	Finance Charge	Total of Payments	Monthly Payments	Annual Percentage Rate
24 mo.	$4,000	$640	$4,640	$193.33	14.68%
36 mo.	$4,000	$960	$4,960	$137.77	14.55%
48 mo.	$4,000	$1,280	$5,280	$110.00	14.35%
60 mo.	$4,000	$1,600	$5,600	$ 93.33	14.12%

As you can see, the rates are quite good. And, if you shop for your loans by mail, you might even be able to shave the percentage a little more. Don't forget, these interest rates are tax deductible. This means that a low-interest loan actually costs you less because of the savings on taxes.

PUTTING YOUR BEST FOOT FORWARD IN YOUR FINANCIAL STATEMENT

Remember, when you make this kind of a loan through the mail, it is still classified as a personal loan. That is, the lender is giving you money strictly on your signature. He is not asking you for any form of security. So, when you plan to use this method, plan ahead very carefully just what you are going to say about yourself.

We are going to give you the details of the kind of questions you will have to answer when you borrow money by mail. To do this, we contacted many of the leading lenders-by-mail and asked them to give us the details of their plans. We have gone over each plan and have summarized the basic information of the questionnaires. With this information, you, the borrower, can be prepared to put your best foot forward when you request a loan by mail. For your convenience, we have divided the questionnaires up into three major categories—personal information, amount of money and kind of credit sought, and a list of your resources and commitments. Of course, each

form varies for each company and some are more compl.
and complete than others, but this is the basic informatio.
required by all. Here's what you will be asked by most of the
firms:

PERSONAL INFORMATION

You will be asked the basic questions of your name, address.
year of birth, number of dependents, previous address, and
number of years at your present address.

All lenders will ask you to give the details of your employment such as job title, length of service, and your approximate
annual income. Some might ask you if your spouse works and
if so, how much he or she earns.

Some will ask you about your insurance coverage. Many of
the companies contacted told us that they do offer very low-
cost life insurance to cover the amount of the loan. The payments for this coverage may be included with the payments on
the actual loan. In most cases, this coverage is optional, and
not required in order to get the loan, but because the cost is
usually quite low, we strongly recommend that you consider
taking the policy with the loan.

AMOUNT OF MONEY REQUIRED AND
KIND OF CREDIT SOUGHT

Some of the loan-by-mail firms will separate their forms into
two parts. One part is to be filled out by the person requesting
the immediate loan of money. The other part is used by the
person who doesn't need the money immediately, but would
like to establish a line of credit for future use.

When you are seeking cash immediately you will be asked to
state the actual amount you want and the number of months
you want to pay it back.

Very few will ask what you plan to do with the money. You
simply fill this out, along with the other information requested,
and your money is sent just as soon as the loan is approved.
There is another important advantage of this kind of loan, and
it is included with most programs offered by the companies:
The loans may be payed back at any time without having to
pay a prepayment penalty.

YOUR RESOURCES AND COMMITMENTS

In this section, the lenders are asking you to tell them where you stand in terms of what you own and what you owe. It is the same sort of information any bank would ask before granting you a personal loan. They will want to know what your annual income is and how you make it. That is, they will want to know what other sources of income you may have, in addition to your job. They will also ask about your expenses—how much rent you pay, the payments on your car, and other regular payments you might be making.

They will also ask about your charge accounts, and other personal loans. Here you will be in excellent shape if you followed the instructions we gave you in Chapter 2. You will have several bank accounts and several loans, all of which will show that you are a person who pays off his loans conscientiously. Of course all your bank references will put you right on top of the "accepted" pile at any mail-order lender.

As we said, each company uses a different questionnaire, some more detailed than others, but they will all want to know this basic information. When you are prepared to answer them with the knowledge we have just given you, and when you are prepared to show these lenders that you are a person to be trusted by the careful way you went about establishing your credit reputation, you will have absolutely no trouble filling out the forms and getting the money you want.

WHERE TO FIND THESE
MONEY-THROUGH-THE-MAIL LENDERS

Every issue of the country's leading business magazines and newspapers carries ads for these mail-order money lenders. Check any issue of *Business Week* and you will see at least five of these companies advertising. Because it would appear that we are endorsing some of them by actually giving names and addresses, we are not able to print them in the pages of this book. But, if you are unable to get a recent issue of *Business Week, The Wall Street Journal,* or any of the other major business publications, you might check with the editors of *The Franklin Letter.* Each month, this publication discusses ways of raising capital, and often lists sources. For details on

this informative monthly newsletter, write to Financial E
The Franklin letter, Box 95, Demarest, New Jersey 07627.
will send you the interesting details of this valuable
publication.

HOW TO FIND THOUSANDS OF LENDERS
READY TO WORK WITH YOU BY MAIL

In addition to these specialized sources of money-through-
the-mail, there are literally thousands of other sources all
across the country ready and anxiously waiting to hear from
you. These people are known by different names in different
parts of the country, but they are for the most part known as
finance brokers and financial consultants. They seldom have
the actual money to lend themselves, but they are constantly
in touch with individuals and companies looking to make good
use of their surplus money. After contacting them, and out-
lining your plans, they will be able to get in touch with many
sources of capital looking for exactly what you have in mind.
When they feel that they have found the right person or company for you, they will get you and the lender together to set
up the deal.

But, you must remember, like you, they too are out to make
money. They make their money in several ways. Some will
charge you a flat fee for the service, some will want a retainer
in advance of any loans, and some will actually take a percentage of the proceeds of the loan they set up in your behalf.

While the cost may be high, it is often the best source of
capital available for a speculative business. But, remember,
these brokers and consultants are carefully scrutinized by the
government and cannot charge you more than the established
rates. In addition, these brokers are all competing with each
other, so you can "shop" for your services by looking for the
best deal. Don't be afraid to wheel and deal when you are
looking for money.

Where can you find these thousands of lenders? Right in the
yellow pages of every telephone directory. And, here's where
the mail service comes in. Go to your local telephone company
business office and tell them that you want to use the yellow
pages for the major financial cities of the country, including

New York, Chicago, San Francisco, Dallas, Boston, and other cities of your choice. They will let you use them in their office and you can copy out all the information you need right there. If they do not have the books you want, just ask and they will order them for you.

Here's a very important fact: If you are already in business, and have a telephone listed as a business telephone, the phone company will get you the copies of the yellow pages you need and give them to you at no charge. You can then have them right in your place of business and use them whenever you have the need.

TAPPING THE KNOW-HOW OF YOUR SUPPLIERS

It is a rare business indeed that handles all of its transactions on a face-to-face basis. Consider the average retail store that stocks a variety of products. In most cases this business with suppliers is done through the mail. And, this can be a tremendous source of short-term capital, if you know how to play it. Let us tell you the story of Gilbert M., a man with an automotive parts store in a midwestern suburb. Gil found himself with accounts payable of about $3,000 each month. Business was good, but he did want money to promote heavily during his busy summer season. He was unable to do what he wanted with the money he was taking in each month, and he already had several small loans with local banks. His bankers were reluctant to loan Gil any more money, and, in fact, Gil was somewhat hesitant about actually borrowing it. When we told him how he could use his trade credit, he was able to have the use of $6,000 for 60 days, and without paying a penny in interest!

GETTING INTEREST-FREE MONEY

Gil wrote to every one of his suppliers, telling of his plans, and giving them a clear picture of his financial condition. What he told them was this: he wanted to extend his regular payments for merchandise to them from his usual 30 days to 60 days, which was all the time he would need to do the promotion during his busy season. Because Gil had been a regular payer, all agreed, and some even offered longer payment. What did this do for Gil?

- It gave him $6,000 to use that he would have had to pay for merchandise;
- It allowed him to get started on his promotion;
- It gave him money on which he did not have to pay any interest;
- While he did not actually do business with any financial institutions, he had negotiated the use of his $6,000 strictly through the mail.
- All of his suppliers were from out of town and a simple letter to each had produced the capital he needed— interest-free.

SOLVING BUSINESS PROBLEMS QUICKLY WITH A POSTAGE STAMP

In many metropolitan centers, various business and service clubs have formed consulting services for the new business-man, and will help either directly, over the phone, or through the mail. In New York City, for example, the Executive Volunteer Corps has been formed. This organization is made up of successful, but retired businessmen who are vitally interested in helping others to make a successful career for themselves. Each has a specialized knowledge and will share it, at no cost, with the beginning businessman.

For information on these excellent sources of professional business talent and free consultation, contact whichever business club exists in your area. This might be the Rotary, the Kiwanis, or any of the many other business-oriented organizations found in both large and small cities. Check with the mayor of your town for the name of the group most likely to help.

ASKING FOR MONEY WITH A LOW-COST AD

Up until now, we have been talking about business organizations of all types that make their money by lending you money —banks, brokers, loan companies, insurance companies, and all the others. But, there are many people in this country with a little extra money that they would like to put to work for themselves. They would like to make more interest on their money than the bank offers, but they are not dabblers in the stock market. You can reach these people for only a few dollars.

Every issue of *The Wall Street Journal, The New York Times,* and the major newspapers in every big city across the country carries special columns on its classified pages. Some are headed "Business Opportunities," others, "Capital Available," and others "Capital to Invest." There is literally a wealth of information and money to be found every day in these columns.

The point is this: for a few dollars, you can often reach thousands of businessmen with your offering in a simple classified ad. Bruce G. wanted to expand a mail-order tie business he was running. He needed capital, but he didn't want to be tied down with a bank loan. He wanted some more flexibility, knowing that his business was highly seasonal. He ran a 17-word ad in a local newspaper, seeking $10,000, and received 12 replies. Of these, three actually offered the money, and he borrowed $5,000 each from two of them. He later found that one of his lenders was a retired department store merchandising expert, and was able to give him a million dollars worth of free advice as well as the cash he needed. Here are some sample ads you might try:

- Will pay ____% interest for $7,500. Well secured and financially sound investment. Contact _____.
- OPPORTUNITY to invest in going business. Need $12,000 and will pay up to ____% interest for six months. Contact _____.
- PARTNER and money needed. Just $5,000 and 10 hours a week will give you 25% of my going fast-food business. Contact _____.
- Make 50% profit for an investment of only $10,000. Going hardware store needs capital to expand. I made this profit when I started the store, you can too. Contact _____.

By all means try your local newspaper first, but don't be afraid to advertise in papers all across the country. People with money to lend are not particularly interested in where they lend it, they just want to know if they will make money on it.

As you can see it is possible and often quite easy to get the money you need by simply walking to your mailbox.

CHECKLIST OF WAYS TO GET MONEY
THROUGH THE MAIL

1. When you borrow money personally, you will not get as much as you could with business loans. Decide to start a low capital business first. You can then take advantage of personal loans through the mail.

2. Check into the loans-by-mail companies for fast, investigation-free loans.

3. Shop for these loans. Each lender is competing with the other and you must make sure you are getting the best deal.

4. Prepare yourself before you file for a loan with the details we gave you on personal information, amount of money and kind of credit sought, and resources and commitments.

5. Check business magazines and newspapers for the names of people who advertise loans through the mail.

6. Find thousands of lenders right in the yellow pages.

7. Be sure to use the credit of your suppliers.

8. Get the help of those who have "been through the mill."

9. Get your money from the classified pages of the newspaper.

7

USING LEVERAGE TECHNIQUES
TO MULTIPLY YOUR WEALTH
AND POWER

Suppose you came across an old pirate's chest half buried in the sand on some forgotten beach. After getting it free, you could hear all the gold pieces clinking around inside. But the chest was locked tight. What would you do?

You'd look around for something to pry off that lid so you could get to all that money, wouldn't you? Of course! In all probability, you'd wind up prying the lid off with some kind of lever—a tool, a crowbar, or a strong piece of wood. You would use "leverage" to get to all that wealth, *fast*. In this case, the lever was the means whereby you opened the lid to riches for yourself.

There's another kind of leverage that can be used today in opening all sorts of financial opportunities for you. It is called *financial leverage*, and it can open up such wealth-producing possibilities that it would take dozens of chests filled with gold to even come close in the amount of dollars waiting there for you.

LEVERAGE—THE SECRET OF TODAY'S
MASSIVE FORTUNES

It would be safe to say that virtually every man who has made his millions during the last twenty years or so has done so with leverage. Leverage is the means whereby a little money controls a great deal of action.

Today, leverage is the pathway to financial success and independence that is open to the little guy, the just-starting wealth-builder, and the smart money man who wants to see his fortunes grow by leaps and bounds.

Basically, leverage means putting up a little of your own money in some deal, getting someone else (a person or an institution) to put up the rest, and you collect the profits. True, you will have to share the profits in some fashion with the owners of all that money you're using. But a piece of a large pie is certainly a lot better than a tiny pie that belongs all to you.

HOW TO MAKE EVERY DOLLAR WORK LIKE TEN

Go back to the lever analogy a moment. With the right lever, you can move a weight ten times heavier than you could without any assistance. With the right financial "lever" you can move ten times as much money as you could if you went into a deal without any help at all. Financial leverage is that simple, and the various ways of applying it are boundless.

How about an example? If you are like so many people who own a home, you probably bought it with a down-payment out of your savings, and have a mortgage for the balance. You can enjoy all the benefits and advantages of living in a comfortable home with relatively little money—someone else (a bank or mortgage company) has come to your assistance with the rest of the money. Your modest savings have been made to act as a lever to get you out of a cramped apartment and into a home of your own. The interest you pay on your mortgage is an added cost to the initial price of the home, but most everyone is more than willing to pay this amount for the long-term advantages this simple financial transaction brings.

It's possible to buy a home at times with only a 10 percent down-payment. With this down-payment, you're able to "control" an investment (your home) costing ten times as much. You've multiplied your financial power ten times. It's that simple.

What most people don't realize is the profit potential in being able to control investments by means of simple leverage techniques. Let's stick with the house example:

1. Let's say you buy a $30,000 house with 10 percent down, or $3,000.

2. During the past years, homes have been increasing at least 10 percent in value every year. Let's say you keep this house three years and then sell.

3. At 10 percent per year, you're now able to sell the house for $40,000.

Question: what is your profit? If you bought for $30,000 and sold for $40,000, you've made $10,000 profit or 33 1/3% on your original $30,000. Right?

Definitely *not!*

Look at this balance sheet and see how leverage has multiplied your money power:

> *Your income:* $40,000 (the sale price of your house)
> *Your expenses:*

> $26,500 to repay original mortgage (remember, you bought a $30,000 house with 10 percent down, or $3,000. The bank loaned you $27,000 as a mortgage. After three years, you've paid off only a small fraction, $500 or so).

> $13,500 balance to you. But, you had other expenses . . .

> $ 4,000 interest paid to the bank during three years, leaving you a balance now of $9,500. You've also paid taxes, maintenance, and other expenses during those three years. Let's assume these would come

to what you would have to pay in rent if you weren't living in a house. Therefore, you can say you've made a clear profit on your house of $9,500. And here's the clincher—you made $9,500 profit on your original investment (down-payment) of only $3,000. That's more than tripling your money in three years. How long would it take for you to become wealthy if you could adapt this same technique to a lot of activities in your life? The pages that follow will show some common ones—you can come up with loads more once you understand the techniques of leverage.

HOW TO MAKE MONEY WHERE YOU LIVE

The previous example of a person buying and selling a home at a profit is a good everyday example of financial leverage. People do it all the time and never think they are speculating. The next step for you, as a serious wealth-builder, is to start doing this deliberately.

Ordinary inflation in home prices puts about 10 percent per year in your pocket for each year that you keep your house. You can boost this percentage several times by doing things to increase the value of your home. Much of this is simple remodeling and decorating, which can add much more to the value of the house without corresponding expense.

That house you paid $30,000 for and later sold for $40,000— what would happen to your profit picture if you had spent an additional $2,000 adding some feature like an extra bedroom? In all probability, you could get an extra $5,000 or a total of $45,000 for that home after three years.

You spent $2,000 to get an extra $5,000. That's another $3,000 profit added to your kitty of $9,500, or $12,500. And, if you let a bank leverage your bedroom addition with a home-improvement loan, you wouldn't even have to put up that $2,000 to make the extra $5,000. All you would pay would be interest on that loan.

Making money where you live—buying, improving, upgrading, and then selling at a profit is one of the best ways to get started in the business of making money using financial leverage. Let's go a step beyond.

HOW TO OWN MORE THAN ONE HOUSE

Let's say you like that house you bought three years ago and don't want to sell it just to collect your profits. Is your wealth-building dream impossible to attain now that all your money is tied down in your house? The answer again is, "No."

Remember the second-mortgage technique we spoke about previously? You can get quite a bit of capital out of your home while you're still living in it. Hank H. was an ex-GI who bought a home for $25,000, with only 10 percent down, when he returned from overseas duty. Five years later, he could have sold it for $38,000 if he just let that old 10 percent per year inflation work for him. But, Hank had put in quite a bit of "sweat equity" into his house.

There were things he did with his own labor that added substantially to the value of the house. In five years, Hank had finished off a basement playroom, a laundry center that would make most women envious, an enclosed breezeway between his house and the garage, and added central air conditioning.

Hank's house was worth every penny of $48,000, and he owed only $21,000 on the original mortgage. Hank had no trouble raising $15,000 on a second mortgage. He chose a second mortgage, rather than a new mortgage for an increased amount for the following reasons:

1. On a new mortgage he would have to pay an increased interest rate on the whole amount.

2. The second mortgage interest rate was high, but he figured his investment plan for the future would enable him to pay it off quickly and thereby pay less interest overall.

FINDING INVESTMENT PROPERTY

Because Hank was handy with tools, he figured he would look for a good house that could be quickly fixed up and resold for a profit. He found one nearby in town. Here's how Hank's financial picture looked after less than a year:

Price of "older" home	$30,000
Down-payment of 33 percent (common on older homes)	$10,000
Mortgage from bank	$20,000

Within a year, Hank had fixed up and sold that house for $42,000. His expenses were as follows:

Remodeling expenses	$ 5,000
Pay off mortgage plus legal fees	$20,000
Total costs	$25,000
Profit (sales price less expenses—$42,000 less costs of $25,000)	$17,000

Now, remember that Hank invested $15,000 that he borrowed on a second mortgage. He has two options open:

1. Pay off the second mortgage and pocket somewhat less than $2,000 as clean profit ($17,000 minus $15,000) or

2. Use that $15,000 second mortgage loan to go after another house deal like the preceding one. In fact, he would really have $17,000 to play with now.

What's the leverage on a deal like this? If you consider that Hank borrowed the $15,000 originally, all he has invested is the interest cost on the second mortgage—let's say $1,000 for a year. That relatively small out-of-pocket expense enables Hank to "control" the $17,000 he made on the house deal. That's a 17-times bit of financial leverage in less than a year!

This kind of money action really made Hank want to go after bigger deals in real estate. He decided to hold on to his $17,000 and make it grow. If one house could prove so profitable—how about four? This is what he did:

1. Surveyed his town and adjoining towns on foot and by

car looking for likely homes he could buy in certain neighborhoods.

2. Spoke at length with building inspectors and zoning officers in the various towns. He found out important facts about minimum lot sizes in various areas, zoning regulations, and the general trend of real estate in various parts of town.

3. Finally bought an old, run-down house on a large lot at a bargain price of $32,000. A lending officer took one look at the house and said "No deal" on a mortgage, but he was interested in Hank's plans.

4. Hank planned to put up half the money, or $16,000. The land on which the old house stood could be used as collateral for a loan of another $16,000. That made the deal possible.

5. Hank bought the property and promptly tore down the old house. He then got a minor subdivision approved and had the large piece of property divided into four building lots.

6. On each of these lots, Hank and a builder he interested in a joint-venture deal put up four homes that were sold for $45,000 each, or $180,000.

7. After all expenses were paid, and profits shared between Hank and the builder according to their respective investments, Hank walked off with $26,000 profit —and this profit still came on the relatively small amount of money he was paying on the second-mortgage interest.

End of year one in Hank's financial history.

CLOSING BIG REAL ESTATE DEALS
WITH LITTLE MONEY

By the start of the second year, Hank was really rolling. He was quite knowledgeable about zoning regulations in various towns, and had a good idea of the various parcels of land on the fringes of town. Like so many areas, his town was a suburb that had grown rapidly after World War II, and by now most land available for residential development had row upon row of houses standing on them. Hank felt the time had come to do some more "homework."

Hank talked with officials at the local Chamber of Commerce, with real estate agents, industrial development officers of the county, and just about every one else who had some "feel" for what was happening in his area. Not surprisingly, he discovered some interesting facts about his area that are repeated in many other areas today:

1. His suburban town attracted people from near-by cities looking for homes, thereby driving up land values immensely;

2. His town had a "pool" of workers, particularly women and older persons who had little job opportunities in a strictly residential town;

3. Several interesting tracts of land were available for industrial development, but most had been snapped up by speculators;

4. Not too far from town, a cantankerous old farmer still tried to scratch a living out of his neglected acres, all the time refusing to sell at a "fair" price to prospective developers.

Here was a situation just ripe for another leverage ploy. Hank came to terms with the farmer and agreed to pay close to his high asking price. But, Hank sewed up the deal with an "option" rather than a lot of money. Most people figured the value of the farmer's land at $100,000 or so. The farmer was asking a cool quarter of a million. Hank got him to come down to $200,000 and put up 10 percent or $20,000 on an option to buy within one year.

HOW LOW COST OPTIONS LET YOU CONTROL BIG PROFIT OPPORTUNITIES

The concept of the option is quite simple. You agree to buy, and the seller agrees to sell a piece of property at a certain price within a certain period of time. In Hank's case, he and the farmer agreed to a sale within one year at $200,000. The farmer could not sell the property to anyone else within that period, regardless of the offer; and Hank had to buy within the year or lose his $20,000 option money. If he bought, the option money became a down-payment, pending final cash settlement.

With this option controlling nearly 80 acres of land, plus

his knowledge of what was happening in his area, Hank went to work. This is what he did:

1. Got an accurate survey of the property, including a topographic and soil and water survey.
2. Hired a firm of architects with considerable experience in industrial development to "rough out" some ideas.
3. Had sketches and plans made of his 80 acres and the way it would look with roads and possible buildings.
4. Incorporated all these designs in an impressive brochure that he had an advertising agency prepare for him.
5. Started a campaign of "selling" his idea for an industrial park to a number of blue-chip companies all over the country.

After mailing 575 brochures and personal letters to as many appropriate corporations he could find, this is what happened:

- 157 replied expressing some interest in the idea, but most were really polite ways of saying "no."
- Of the 157, there were thirteen fairly serious expressions of interest in the idea.
- Of the thirteen, three prospects really looked "hot."

Hank went after the thirteen prospects and paid particular attention to the three hot prospects. Within six months, he had negotiated his first sale of a parcel of property together with a building he agreed to build for the client on a sale and lease-back arrangement.

With one sure sale, others came quickly. Before a year was up, Hank exercised his option and bought the land from the farmer which was really a "bargain" by now. With his knowledge of putting together a deal like this, several banks were competing to offer Hank the money he needed to develop the property.

At the end of the second year of his use of financial leverage, Hank was worth a quarter of a million dollars and the prospects were virtually certain he would become a millionaire in very short order.

HOW TO MAKE MONEY IN OFFICE BUILDINGS AND SHOPPING CENTERS

By now you should have a good idea of how leverage works in the building field, and particularly how an ordinary guy like Hank was able to parlay a modest initial investment in his own home into a substantial fortune. We spent much time on Hank's experiences because we earnestly feel his good fortune can be repeated over and over again in various parts of the country. The reason is simple: the country is growing; the population is growing; and business is growing to meet all the needs of a growing society. In addition to homes and factories, we will need much more office space, shopping centers, and apartment houses in the years to come. And, you can become wealthy supplying these needs for a growing America.

Shopping centers, office buildings, and high-rise apartments can make money for you *fast,* provided you keep in mind these principles:

1. Don't figure on making money as a "landlord"—the headaches of managing the projects will keep you from swinging other deals.

2. Don't start building until you've got a lot of advance leases signed—you'll find financing the project incredibly easy if you can flash signed leases to a banker.

3. Don't figure on owning the project for any length of time—you'll make more money if you sell out within a few years.

Here now is the reason behind this set of money-making principles in the big leagues of real estate development.

A lot of people think owning an apartment house would be the height of financial success. Just think: all those rents coming in each month, as regular as clockwork ... a nice, rent-free apartment to live in ... the prestige of ownership, etc. Don't believe it. Running an apartment house, an office building, or shopping center is a job, just like running any other business. If you want to hold onto the property, look for a property manager to handle all the details of leases, negotiating, rent collection, maintenance, and operation of the property.

You will find in many cases that the rents coming in (your cash flow) will just about cover your expenses, costs of operation, and depreciation. Seldom will you ever find the property earning a surplus that you can pocket as a "salary" for your work. The profit comes only on *resale* in which you have a built-in tax advantage.

HOW TO MAKE REALLY BIG MONEY BY SELLING YOUR PROPERTY

Thomas Y. went this route. He saw a need for offices in a near-by suburb and talked to businessmen whose offices were then located in the overcrowded city. Armed with enough commitments for future rentals, Thomas was able to swing a million-dollar deal with borrowed money. But, let the actual money details develop this success story:

- The building Thomas planned cost a cool million. With only 10 percent, most of which was already borrowed, he was able to finance the rest.

- Once the building was up, and the businesses for which he had signed leases in advance had moved in, Thomas was collecting about $100,000 a year in rents.

- His annual expenses were in the neighborhood of $35,000, and he figured his depreciation at about $55,000 annually.

- This left Thomas with a total profit of only $10,000 on his million-dollar deal. ($35,000 plus $55,000 equals $90,000; from an income of $100,000, he had $10,000 left.)

Not very much after swinging a million-dollar deal, is it? Yet, this is a typical balance sheet for such a project. But, let's see where Thomas actually turned his small annual profits into real wealth:

- At the end of five years, the demand for building space had driven the value of the $1,000,000 building up to a figure of $1,500,000 (remember that old 10 percent per year inflation working for you?)

- Cost of Thomas's project is down to $725,000.

($1,000,000 less five years depreciation at $55,000 a year or $275,000.)

- Total profit to Thomas is $775,000. (Sale price of $1,500,000 minus his unrecovered cost of $725,000.)

Now, the most important thing to remember is that this $775,000 represents *capital gains* and it is taxed at a much lower rate than ordinary income. This averages out to an "income" of $155,000 a year in a low tax bracket. This is where Thomas made his money, and you can readily see just what magic lies in the secret of leverage.

Many businesses forecast their needs in office space years in advance. For this reason, you can presell corporations on space in a yet-to-be-built office building. You agree on rentals and sign leases. These leases are almost as good as money when it comes to borrowing funds to build the project. Again, the leases are really the "levers" you use to move vast amounts of money.

HOW TO USE FRANCHISING AS A LEVERAGE TOOL

Franchising as a business has had its ups and downs during the years. Some people have even said the heyday of profit making in the field has passed. Don't you believe it! A study some time ago showed that various franchising operations contributed almost 10 percent of the Gross National Product. That means $100 *billion* dollars if we figure out current GNP at $1 trillion or so. As we become more and more a service-oriented economy, more and more services will be needed, from fast food chains to income tax services. And all of these services can benefit from a franchise operation.

What is franchising? As simply as possible, a franchise operation is a relatively small business that belongs to a "family." It shares the family's name, reputation, and secrets of operation.

The family company—the corporation that owns the image and everything else connected with the business name, is the *franchisor*. The local businessman, running the operation, is the *franchisee*.

The reason franchising has become so big is simple: *two-way leverage.*

The *franchisor* enjoys tremendous financial leverage. The *franchisee* puts up the starting money and finances the rest locally, with the *franchisor* sharing in the profits. The *franchisor* also has an independent businessman running a business on his own and benefits from the attention that such a person gives to his investment.

The *franchisee* enjoys leverage, too. He can draw upon all the experience the *franchisor* has accumulated in making the business successful. In addition, being connected with a national franchise chain usually makes it easier for the franchisee to get local financing. The banks know that a lot of the risks in starting a new business are eliminated in a franchise operation.

You can make a considerable amount of money as a *franchisee* if you want to invest your money that way. You will enjoy quite a bit of leverage and probably make out better than if you put your capital into a business of your own. However, the big money is to be made in *selling* franchises. In other words, we're suggesting you think about becoming the *franchisor.*

HOW TO START A FRANCHISE OPERATION

There is no pat answer to this question. Today, there are probably a hundred different products or services sold under various franchises. The important thing is to build a *success package.* To do this, you will need to:

1. Start a business that has wide potential throughout the country. In other words, stay away from such a specialized product or service that you can't sell it readily in other parts of the country.

2. Make your initial business a real showcase of success —something that you can show off to potential franchisees as a proven money maker.

Once you've accomplished the jobs just described, your career as a *franchisor* begins. This means you have to sell other businessmen on the idea of joining your bandwagon and duplicating the success you have achieved. There are two ways of doing this:

- You can sell the franchises yourself. This means an awful lot of legwork on your part, and your first sale will probably be slow in coming. Generally speaking, after the first few "tough" sales are made, the rest come more easily. A "snowballing" effect takes place as one after another successful places carrying your name are opened up.

- You can let a commercial franchising service organization take over. For a fee they will sell and service your franchises. Many will even give you advice on polishing your success package to make it even more saleable to potential franchisees.

After you've made a success of your own potential franchise business, get some solid legal advice on how to protect your ideas in a franchising operation. There are many types of franchises, and many ways of sharing the profits, so no one piece of advice we could give could possibly cover all situations.

Within these pages, it is impossible to tell you everything about starting a franchising operation, but we have touched upon some basic principles, and refer you to more complete information in the books and publications found in most libraries.

DISCOVERING LEVERAGE IN THE STOCK MARKET

There are a few people who were smart enough to buy blocks of today's glamour stocks, and then wait ten or twenty years for the companies to grow spectacularly and make them rich. Someone calculated that if you had invested $5,000 in Xerox twenty years ago, you would be worth several millions of dollars today. Since you don't want to wait a generation to become rich, what *do* you do?

Leverage! That same magic works in the stock market and it is the means whereby hundreds of millionaires are being made today.

In our previous chapter we explained a relatively simple leverage tool of buying stock on margin, then using the stock to borrow more money, and so on. There are many other ways of using leverage in the stock market that would take volumes to explain. Here is just one simple example of leverage:

Many companies whose stock is actively traded have "warrants" outstanding. A warrant gives the owner the right to buy the stock of the company at a specified price. Warrants are traded in the market just like stocks and their values go up and down with market conditions. Their leverage potential is fantastic, if you pick the right company.

USING WARRANTS TO LEVER YOUR WAY TO WEALTH

The best way to explain this concept is with the following example:

- Company ABC's stock is currently trading at $30 per share.
- There are warrants outstanding that permit the holder to buy shares of ABC's stock at $33 per share. The warrants are being traded at $3 each.
- If you bought the warrant at $3, and then used it to buy stock at $33 per share, your cost per share would be $36. (We're neglecting broker's commissions for simplicity.)
- But, you can buy shares of ABC's stock for only $30 a share on the open market—where's the profit?

The profit lies in the leverage possibilities as the stock of ABC Company goes up. True, you could buy ABC stock and make your profit on the stock, but the warrants give you so much more financial muscle. Claude R. dabbled with a small amount of cash and actually doubled his money. Here's just how Claude did it:

- Claude bought 100 warrants at $3 each for a total investment of $300.
- In less than a year, the price of ABC stock went up to $40.
- Claude immediately exercised the rights of the warrants and bought 100 shares at only $33 a share.
- He immediately resold the shares he bought and made a profit of $7 a share, or a total of $700.

- Because his initial investment was only $300, his profit was $400, more than doubling his money in less than a year.

If you had invested that same $300 in shares of stock selling at $30, you could have purchased only ten shares. Each share rose $10 in a period of a year, so your profit with shares would have only been $100. Quite a difference!

Different leverage techniques can be applied to the various kinds of stocks issued and traded on the Big Board. Brokers can tell you about such operations as "Puts" and "Calls"— leveraging operations that enable you to control large blocks of stock with relatively little money. It must be admitted that there is much more speculative risk in these types of leveraging operations than in the building and land businesses we described in more detail. But, if you crave real big-money action, you can find it in the market.

HOW TO CASH IN ON COMMODITIES

Another aspect of levering is the commodity market. This is something like the stock market, but some of the rules are different. This difference in rules make large gains possible on little investment. It also means you can be wiped out just as easily.

Commodities are things like wheat, butter, eggs, rubber, tin, pork, and a host of other commodities of trade that are bought and sold. They are sold by means of standard "contracts" that are traded through recognized commodity brokers. The important thing is that you usually have to put only 10 percent down to buy a contract. For example:

- You "buy" a contract for $5,000 worth of a certain commodity. This commodity will be ready for delivery some time in the future.

- This contract can be bought for only $500—the rest is financed.

- You hope that by the time the commodity is ready for delivery, the marketprice will have risen so you can make a profit.

- If the market goes up only 10 percent (and larger swings are not unusual in the volative commodity market) your contract is worth $5,500. You sell at $5,500, pay off the $4,500 you borrowed, and make a neat $1,000. Again, in a couple of months you've doubled your money. Leverage and its magic work again!

CHECKLIST OF LEVERAGE TECHNIQUES YOU CAN USE

We hope by now you have some idea of the enormous power available when you use financial leverage. In your quest for wealth, you will surely discover other ways of using this powerful tool to your advantage. What we have set out to do was to show you some of the more common methods employed by successful people in the past and demonstrate principles that will guide you in your own operations. Review some of them now:

- Leverage is just about the only practical means of quickly building a fortune from scratch. Therefore, in every business deal, you should search out the underlying leverage principle. Look for the place where a little force (your investment) will move a lot of money (someone else's).

- Your own home is a good starting place to apply the simple principle of leverage. This doesn't mean you have to run out and sell your house right now. But it does mean you have a headstart on a fortune if you've lived in it for a couple of years or so.

- Get to know your area. Survey your locality looking for opportunities in raw land, real estate, old home conversions, etc. Get to know your banker, real estate man, and town officials.

- Study the growth history and potential of your area. Know what is likely to happen to people and where they work. In this way you can plan intelligently for stores, shopping centers, office buildings, or high-rise apartments.

- If you don't have money immediately, try swinging a deal with an option. Then get out and hustle! Make plans with the help of a professional and try to presell space or leases. This will give you the financing you need to swing big deals.

- Franchising can be a powerful two-way leverage tool once you've started a successful business. This is one of the fastest ways a small business can grow big overnight. Having 100 semi-independent owners run stores sharing a part of the profit with you will make more money for you—with less work—than trying to run just ten stores yourself.

- The stock and commodity markets will always present opportunities for smart people to become wealthy with leverage techniques. The beginner should do a lot of homework before entering this arena.

8

HOW TO ACQUIRE
BUSINESS REAL ESTATE AT
LITTLE OR NO COST

You've made up your mind to be independent and rich in a business of your own. Now you've got to find a place to work. Most of the opportunities we've described so far require little or no space. In time, however, you'll find that you need office space, storage space, or other types of business real estate to carry on your business most effectively. In particular, once you start talking seriously to bankers and other lenders, they'll want to visit your business location just to see your kind of operation. Let's face it, the best idea in the world doesn't look very exciting or promising over the dining room table.

In this chapter we will show you various ways of acquiring the business real estate you need with little or no investment. We will show you how you can "borrow" the real estate you need to get started, and how you can make deals that will enable you to use the property you need on terms most advantageous to you.

SURVEYING YOUR TRUE REAL ESTATE NEEDS

While we think it's important for you to have a regular, professional location to conduct your affairs, don't make the mistake of opening an expensive office the instant you decide to go into business. The smart thing to do is to survey your true needs before you get started. Here are some questions to ask yourself that will keep you from getting in trouble with an unwise or too costly a lease:

- Does my business require large amounts of storage space?
- What about machines, equipment, or supplies? How much room will normal day-to-day supplies need?
- Are there any zoning restrictions that will hinder my operations in the location I have in mind?
- Should I operate in the beginning from my home or from a mailbox?
- Will I be getting a lot of business visitors, business calls by suppliers, or other traffic?
- Do I need a "prestige" location to impress customers, or will a place in the low-rent district of town serve equally well?

Other questions will, no doubt, occur to you once you start thinking about your requirements. The important thing is not to let the excitement of going into business make you blind to the realities of the situation. Nothing can be more discouraging than to have a poor month in which little money has come in and then to have to write a whopping big rent check to the landlord.

Here are two hints that others have found quite valuable. Follow them and you will not go far wrong, ever:

1. Write down all your needs—in other words, the answers to the kinds of questions we've suggested above.
2. Don't settle for anything that falls far outside of your true business needs.

For example: you may have decided that your operation

does not need expensive office space. It's a mail-order operation that needs storage space and convenience to the post
office as primary requirements, let's say. A brand-new office
building goes up in town. Resist the temptation to sign a lease
on that impressive new office . . . forget the view . . . the fancy
office . . . and the carpeted reception area outside. None of
these will help you pay the rent, and will be a discouraging
drain on your resources in the beginning. There will be plenty
of time for the "fancy trimmings" when you hit the big money.

STARTING WITH AN OFFICE AT HOME

Unless you have an idea for a manufacturing operation that
will require a factory type of location, or a retail store, it is
often possible to test your business ideas by starting it in your
home on a temporary basis. Here are some advantages when
starting:

- You already pay for your home; it costs nothing extra
  to start a business from your kitchen or your basement;

- You can start and stop as you please—there are no
  leases or other commitments to worry about;

- It's very easy for a spare-time operation—you don't
  have to go off to business to another location.

- And finally, using your home for business enables you
  to take advantage of certain tax breaks the Government gives to businessmen. You can deduct portions
  of the expenses of running your home if you use it for
  business, even if it is part-time. The exact amount
  depends on how much you use and how often. But, in
  any case, the amount can be worthwhile.

  Jack S., a builder we know, used his own home as
a "model home." Whenever he got a prospect for a
custom-built home, Jack would invite the prospect to
his house and show him all the features he could expect
in his own home. It was a showplace for construction
features and decorations, and the government allowed
him to deduct the cost of this home from the expenses
of running the business. Imagine, even getting the lawn
mowed was a tax deduction!

But, before you let the above advantages of running a business from your home convince you, you should take note of certain *disadvantages*. You may decide it would really be better to rent (or "borrow" as we will show you) right from the beginning.

- It can be tough to work and to concentrate at home. The family, particularly in a small home, can be a source of annoyance and constant interruptions.

- Many times space is so tight, you have to spend time "setting up and taking down" every time you want to work.

- Often, it's impossible to use space most efficiently when you work at home.

- Finally, make sure any money you decide to spend to equip an office at home is well spent. For example: you decide to add an office wing to your present home at a cost of $10,000. It might be wiser to rent a location for a couple of years which will wind up costing you less than the $10,000. What happens at the end of a couple of years if you need more space to expand? If you rented space, you could simply move to larger quarters. If you built an office on your home, you might find it impossible to expand later on and you would have to rent anyway. But now, you're burdened with an office at home you can't use and probably can't rent to anyone else.

No hard and fast rules can be given other than to spend some time asking and answering the kinds of questions we've posed here. Generally speaking, however, the beginner will usually find it to his advantage to start a kitchen-table operation and then move out as soon as the business shows it can "pay the rent."

One other rule should be observed: keep records of everything you spend on your home—repairs, heat, light, water, etc., starting from the first day you use your home for business. Records like this will be immensely valuable when tax time comes around and you want to document your expenses.

RENT-FREE PROPERTY CAN BE YOURS

There are a number of ways you can acquire the use of property and not have to pay rent at all, or only a small fraction of what similar space would rent for. It all revolves about keeping your eyes open and taking advantage of special situations. In a nutshell—you have to show the landlord, or whoever controls the property, that your intended use will cause it to be more profitable, or will save the owner money or work. Let's look at some examples:

Case 1 Bill S. had an idea for a business that would serve the advertising industry. He planned on becoming an "art broker." In the advertising business there are artists who specialize in different types of subjects: some are good with fashion illustration, others are good at detailed technical illustrations, and others concentrate in dozens of areas in between. Bill planned on lining up a number of artists and photographers with varied talents and specialties, and acting as their agent in selling their services to advertising agencies, advertisers, picture services, and the like. Bill needed space to carry on his work—room for sample portfolios of artists' work, telephone services, and conference space to bring artist and client together for meetings. How did he do this?

Actually, Bill solved his problem quickly and easily. He merely discussed his idea with a large advertising agency that would probably become one of his clients once he started. They had constant need for various types of art services. Bill and the agency worked out this deal: the agency would give Bill space in one part of their art department, at no cost, if Bill would give them first crack at the artists he planned to handle in his business. All Bill had to do was pay out-of-pocket expenses for the phone, messenger services, and the like. Both Bill and the agency had something to gain in this deal:

- *The advertising agency* had a number of different accounts. The art director often had to spend a long time calling in and interviewing different free-lance artists and photographers for specific assignments. With Bill's operation at his elbow in his art department, he could quickly size up an artist's talent for a particular job and have Bill handle all the details. This saving in time was worth the cost of the office space several times over each month.

- *The art broker,* Bill S., had obvious gains. He had free office space, use of all the agency's facilities, such as the receptionist and meeting rooms, and an inside track onto all the agency's art business.

Case 2 George W. had plans for opening a lettershop. He would handle simple printing with a small offset press, maintain customer mailing lists, address statements and promotion pieces, and do all the other jobs normally associated with a lettershop operation. From the point of view of convenience in moving supplies in and finished work out, George reasoned a first-floor store location would be his best choice. Eventually, when he became successful, he could lease a large industrial type of location to handle his volume. But, for the time being, a storefront would work best. Neither would he need a location in a high rent district, or an expensive shopping district to attract window shoppers. His operation, even though handled from a store, did not depend on walk-in traffic for business. Again, the solution to George's space problems came about rather simply once George surveyed the situation. Here's what he did:

George looked carefully at several towns adjoining a rapidly growing shopping center on the main highway. Most of these towns had old-fashioned "Main Streets" that were increasingly hard hit by the competition of the shopping center. Many of the old stores were vacant; vandalism was becoming a problem here and there.

Almost singlehandedly, George was able to reverse this trend. He picked out a likely location and talked to the owner of the empty store. He would be glad to establish his business in the store, maintain the area, do minor repairs as needed, and discourage vandals by keeping a lighted area, if the store owner would let him have the place rent-free. The owner readily agreed. After all, he was collecting no rent on an empty store, and the prospects of ever renting it again seemed quite dim. A tenant such as George would do a lot toward encouraging other tenants to move in and would also preserve the land-lord's investment by preventing further deterioration. The deal was quickly made and George had a place for his business rent-free.

Case 3 Henry R. came from a very poor background and always wanted to own a string of apartment houses. As a child, Henry grew up with the image of a landlord as being the wealthiest kind of person on the face of the earth. Imagine—each month he drove up in a big new car, called on all the tenants in the building, and went away with pockets bulging with money. What a dream!

When Henry grew up he tried to make that dream come true. But, with little capital resources, Henry would be hard-pressed to swing the down-payment on a modest house for himself and his family. An apartment house deal seemed com-pletely out of the question. That is—until Henry did a little looking and discovered this interesting fact:

Henry revisited his old neighborhood and a few people still remembered him. But now the old neighborhood had changed drastically for the worst. The old apartment houses had all become the worst kind of slum—filthy, in utter disrepair, and filled with frustrated people. Slumlords had made what money they could on the properties and now had abandoned them. Even simple services were not available to the tenants.

Henry did some checking and discovered that the nominal owners of these properties were mortgage companies who acquired the properties because the previous owners defaulted on their loans. Henry visited the loan officer of one of these mortgage companies and offered the following deal:

He would take over ownership and responsibility for the properties in question—in effect, Henry would be the legal owner of the properties without the encumbrance of mort-gages. Both parties would stand to gain in such a situation.

- The mortgage companies had no hope of ever recover-ing their money invested in the property. Instead, each day they were forced to hold on to the properties in-creased their headaches. Besides, from a tax point of view, the buildings had been written off.

- Henry profited in two ways. First, he immediately became the owner of these buildings and legally entitled to collect whatever rents were available. But, coming from the neighborhood himself, he understood the people in the area and was able to establish a different relationship with them. Instead of being a slumlord out to exploit them, the people looked upon Henry as one of their own—a friend who was genuinely interested in upgrading the property. Within months, the first apartment Henry took over began to take on a new appearance. Not being saddled with an impossible mortgage, he was able to put more of his rents into repairs. His tenants appreciated this and began taking care of the property more than they ever did before. In time, Henry became the owner of a half dozen run-down tenements and apartments and had transformed them into well-kept, decent housing units that brought him a profit for his time and work month in and month out.

What do these three case histories reveal to you? More than anything, they demonstrate that you can acquire substantial business real estate in return for things other than money. You can find office space, business locations, even money-earning rental properties if you will only be on the lookout for opportunities. Again, no hard and fast rules can be given to guarantee you the same kind of opportunities discovered by the three persons whose histories we've related. However, you can use these general rules to help you uncover such deals:

1. Look for the owners of properties that you can use and see if you can discover what special needs or problems they face in the ownership of these properties.

2. Try to find a way of solving their problems in such a way that you can either use the property at no cost, or own it without making a large investment of your capital. The examples show just three ways it has been done. There are hundreds of others.

HOW THE TAX COLLECTOR CAN HELP YOU
FIND WHAT YOU NEED

The local tax collector can be a fruitful source of leads to properties that are available at less than their market value. Get to know him, and make sure you read the legal notices in your paper. The fine print in these notices hide a tremendous amount of opportunity for someone who knows how to go after them.

Seldom is valuable business property available at a tax sale. In other words, don't expect to buy a factory complete with machinery for practically nothing. The machinery and tools are usually disposed of at an auction (and bargains are available here if you have the money to buy in large lots) and the property is usually sold before the tax man can take over.

Instead, tax sales are usually the result of such factors as:

- Someone owns a real "white elephant" as far as property goes. After a period, maintenance becomes so great that the property is simply abandoned. In time, the tax man takes it over for unpaid taxes;

- An owner of a property dies and heirs are not immediately discovered. Again, after a time, the tax man takes over the property for back taxes;

- A land development company puts on a high-pressure sales campaign and sells a quantity of building lots in some undeveloped area. There are hundreds of owners, many of whom live out of state and never even look at their property. If the land development company goes bankrupt (and this has happened in innumerable instances) the land is not developed until perhaps many years later by someone else. A careful search will reveal that many of the previous owners, discouraged with their investment, have simple let it go by the boards. Years later, the tax man owns the property for back taxes and it's available at auction.

Many more instances can be revealed showing how property can accrue to the tax collector for nonpayment of taxes. The important thing to keep in mind is this: even at an auction, you will pay a decent price for property being sold for unpaid taxes. In other words, don't expect to buy a $40,000 home for a couple of thousand dollars of unpaid back taxes. Where you can make money working with your tax man is by *anticipation*.

Here is a case in point. Years ago, a major land development company acquired a large tract of land near a big city. Preliminary surveys indicated a bridge and a major highway system would pass right through this tract. Accordingly, the land company sold hundreds of small lots to private investors as a means of speculating. Once the bridge and highway were built, the land values would undoubtedly increase twenty to fifty times. As things turned out, the bridge was finally located a mile or two south of the original location and the highways missed the tract completely.

Years later, most of these investors had either completely forgotten about these lots or had abandoned them by neglecting to pay taxes. Sensing a building boom that was growing out from the surrounding area, Jim S. did a little digging through tax records. He got a plot plan of the area from the tax collector and colored in the areas that were owned by the town for nonpayment of taxes. With another color, he indicated lots that were still privately owned. He discovered a curious thing, something very common in situations such as this. Years ago, small lots were permitted and most of the lots sold by the land development company were twenty and forty foot properties. Today, the town had upgraded the zoning of the area and a minimum of 80 feet was needed. With these two facts, Jim set to work as follows:

- He wrote to the owners of the properties, advising them that the lots were all undersized and offered them options to buy the property at a specified price before a certain date in the future.

- He petitioned the tax collector to put up adjoining properties for sale at public auction. Since Jim had options on adjoining properties, no one was interested in bidding on the undersized lots that were being put up for sale. As a result, Jim was able to buy them for the low minimum price established by the tax office.

- Jim interested a builder in a joint venture. Together, they exercised the options that Jim had acquired and were soon the owners of valuable real estate that met all the zoning requirements for the area. All told, some forty homes were built at an average profit of $6,000 to $8,000 per home. That meant that Jim and his builder-partner shared a total profit of nearly $300,000.

BARGAINS FROM YOUR FRIENDLY SHERIFF

In the previous pages, we have been talking about sales through the office of the tax man. Actually, these sales are usually conducted by the sheriff in many states and you can find out from his office what is being put up for sale. In addition to tax sales, the sheriff usually is responsible for selling the properties of bankrupts and other insolvencies. Again, you should keep close tabs either by visiting the sheriff's office, or by making it a habit to read the fine print of legal notices that appear regularly in local papers.

HOW TO PROFIT FROM GOVERNMENT LAND SALES AND LEASES

The Federal Government, and state governments to a lesser extent, are among the largest landowners in the country. Because the Government really means you, and everyone else in the country, this land actually belongs to all of us. Various laws, some dating back to the early days of our country, have been enacted to give everyone a fair chance to enjoy this land in one form or another.

Much of the land belonging to the Federal Government consists of areas in the far West. This land is used not only for recreation, but is also leased out to timber companies for lumbering operations. This is a well-known example of the use of public lands by private companies, but—did you know that you, as a private individual, can enjoy similar benefits?

For example: the old Homestead Act, enacted a century ago, is still in effect. If you agree to live and work on certain tracts belonging to the Government, you will receive title to the land after a number of years. You invest your time and work: the land is given to you free and clear.

The wealth builder who is using the various borrowing techniques we have been describing in this book should not overlook all the things available from the Government—land, money, advice, publications, and a host of other helpful aids. Many of these sources will be covered in a separate chapter later on. The important things at this point is to keep firmly in mind the idea that the Government is right there in back of you, ready to help you on your journey to wealth.

PRESERVING YOUR CAPITAL

Some form of business real estate will eventually be necessary once you start rolling in a business venture of your own. It may be as simple as a home office in one corner of your living room, or a vast manufacturing plant. We have tried to show you some of the many techniques available to you for acquiring the space you need, and even investment property, without putting out any money at all. In some cases, you can get by by putting up only a small fraction of the value of the property, as, for example, when you adopt the techniques of property options previously described.

All of what we have said can be summarized in this basic principle; keep it in mind constantly and you will be surprised at how many deals you will uncover:

> *You can gain the use of property, and sometimes outright ownership, if you can show the owner that your intended use will bring him some benefit he does not now enjoy. If the benefit is big enough (and some of our case histories demonstrated that) you can get the use of the property for nothing.*

CHECKLIST FOR MAKING REAL ESTATE AND PROPERTY DEALS

- Don't act hastily in renting or leasing business premises; with a little work, you could get the space you need *free.*
- Usually you're better off, as a beginner in business, if you can start from an office at home.
- Try to "graduate" quickly to a full-time, outside loca-

tion when your business income warrants it; you'll find it easier to get loans and to attract other investors.

- Get a sharp pencil and figure carefully the advantages and disadvantages of renting or buying business property. Generally speaking, you'll probably find that renting will help you preserve capital and give you tax advantages to boot.

- Remember the techniques of using options to control parcels of real estate. For all practical purposes, you can consider yourself the owner of the parcel and work out profitable deals with developers, investors, etc.

- In every situation, see what you have to trade off to make a better deal. Often, you can trade free use of property *today* for a piece of the profit *tomorrow*. This is the most important thing to keep in mind if you want to get the property you need without investing all your money in land or buildings.

9

PROFIT FROM EQUIPMENT OWNED BY OTHERS

"Just look at that press! It turns out 4,000 impressions an hour. And that cutter over there can actually be programmed to do any job in the shop. Those two folders in the next room will keep up with any press made and they can do wonders with a sheet of paper."

The man doing the talking had recently started his own commercial printing business, and we were being given the grand tour of his very impressive operation. Enjoying his role as host and reflecting obvious pride, he continued to show us his modern building and equipment. His office machines were just as impressive as the production machinery. And, his building was soundly built and carefully planned for productivity.

Bill M. had worked hard for others for most of his life. He had pinched and saved until the big day when he opened his own business. And, it was truly something to see. We have seldom seen better planned plants, and the equipment was first rate. But, unlike many other businessmen who find themselves in a similar situation, Bill had avoided the temptation to own everything in sight. He had seen several of his friends go into heavy debt to buy the equipment that decorated their plants, only to end up short of the cash needed to buy supplies needed for a day-to-day operation. Bill would have liked to tell his friends that he "owned" all of his equipment, but he knew that this was a small reward compared to the long-range benefits he would have from *not* owning his equipment. And, as far as his customers were concerned, it didn't make a bit of difference whether he owned the equipment or not. It was the service that was important to them.

AVOIDING THE "DANGERS" OF OWNERSHIP

When Bill first thought of going into business for himself, he, too, wanted to own everything outright. But, he had seen what had happened to some of his friends who had gone this route. They had the equipment and they could brag that they owned it, but all it did was sit quietly in their plants. With every cent tied up in machinery, these men had been unable to buy the paper and supplies needed to carry on the routine of business, and many had closed in a very few months. They had been completely stymied by the lack of working capital because they wanted to own their equipment.

But, Bill had discovered that by leasing he could have all the equipment he needed to start his business, and still retain most of his cash to use in building the business.

HOW TO GET PROPERTY AND EQUIPMENT WITH NO CASH OUTLAY

Leasing is an almost magic way to keep your cash intact. Any businessman who leases equipment, buildings, land, machinery, and even patents is actually borrowing money from the owners of these things—and most important, he will still have most of the cash he started with.

When you acquire the *use* of property through a lease, it is just the same as borrowing the *value* of the property. The only difference is this: it does not show up as an asset on your balance sheet. It does show up as a fixed expense and appears much the same as a long-term debt.

HOW TO USE THIS TECHNIQUE TO INSURE THAT YOUR EQUIPMENT WILL ALWAYS MAKE MONEY FOR YOU

Just about anything you can lease can be supplied with a maintenance contract. Maintenance is not always included, and you must be sure to check the contract carefully if you want this feature. Depending on the kind of equipment you lease, and what the chances are of it needing regular repair, maintenance can be of value.

Morton H., a man who has five salesmen on the road with company cars, has always taken advantage of the maintenance clause in his auto leasing contracts. Because the cars are used heavily, and because time is money, Morton negotiated a contract that gives his men an immediate replacement for a car in need of repairs. This is important; when he has a man off the road, Morton is not making money.

Another feature of leasing that Morton found to be important with his fleet of cars was the fact that his costs were always fixed and predictible. He knew to the penny how much each car was going to cost him each year. Even though the cars often were damaged and required extensive repairs, Morton's costs stayed the same. Of course, Morton was gambling with the leasing company. He could have bought the cars for less than he was actually paying in total for leasing, and taken his chances on the repair and replacement costs. But, over the years, Morton found that the leasing arrangement with a maintenance clause was his best bet.

When a businessman considers installing large machinery, it is often necessary to include provision for an on-site maintenance man. This maintenance man may spend six months reading the newspaper before a major breakdown takes place. And all that time, he is collecting a salary. But, when a piece of equipment is leased, it is also possible to include a maintenance agreement with the lease. If the leasing company is lax in sending a maintenance man over, it is a simple matter to withhold the monthly payment. Results take place quickly when this is done.

HOW TO MAKE SURE YOUR EQUIPMENT WILL NEVER BECOME OBSOLESCENT

In some areas of industry, equipment becomes obsolete almost overnight. The computer field serves as a good example. Developments in equipment take place at such a rapid pace that unused equipment is often out of date before it even moves from the factory to the customer's location. When this is a problem, it is often possible to write a clause in the leasing agreement that insures that as your requirements change in relation to new equipment available, the new equipment will be substituted for the current rental.

UNCLE SAM HELPS YOU PAY FOR NEEDED MACHINERY

Whether you buy or lease, you will be able to get tax help for much of the equipment you use. When you buy, you get depreciation allowances for your equipment that go to reduce some of the taxes you pay. However, these deductions are always set up for a specified time period, and usually get less and less each year.

With a leasing arrangement, you can take tax deductions forever. While we cannot possibly hope to give you all the facts to consider in every case, there are two general rules that you can follow. They are:

- After carefully considering the anticipated life of the machine or property, and all of the costs involved, your decision should be made on the basis of taxes saved.

- Generally speaking, the cost of a leased machine will be greater than the cost of the same machine purchased outright. But remember this important fact: you will always have the cash available for working capital when you lease your equipment.

This is one case where the tax laws are pretty clear. However, should you decide to go the purchased equipment route, you must be prepared to keep a very careful set of depreciation records for the tax people. This can also be an expense and should be considered when you make your decision.

USING THE SALE-LEASEBACK, THE MILLIONAIRE'S SECRET

One of the fastest ways of raising capital when you already own property is through the sale-leaseback deal. It's really quite simple, but let's explain it as it happened to Fred D., the owner of a small sheet metal shop.

Fred was just about making ends meet. He had been in business about ten years, but still found himself down at the plant Saturdays and Sundays. Fred was not a compulsive worker—he was simply strapped for the capital needed to hire someone to relieve him of these chores and to expand the business to a point where it would be more profitable.

Fred, by this time, owned all of his equipment. He had gone the purchase and depreciation route, and it was all his. He also owned the building, too. He had considered remortgaging the building, but found that for what he would get, it really wasn't worthwhile. Then, he discovered the sale-leaseback. He could sell his physical assets to a company that would then lease them back to him at a fair rate. Most of the companies that do this are institutional investors such as life insurance companies. In Fred's case, he found a small investment group that was willing to take a chance on a smaller operation. They bought everything, and gave Fred a long-term net lease. Fred had to agree to stay in business, and to stay in the building for a long period of time, but he was planning to do that anyway. In addition to the lease payments, Fred had to agree to pay the taxes and insurance. But it was worth it to get his hands on the capital that allowed him to buy his Saturdays and Sundays, plus the promise of rapid expansion with his ready cash.

Here are the advantages of the sale-leaseback:

- Large amounts of cash are immediately freed to be used for whatever purpose.
- Money is no longer tied up in real estate and equipment.
- There are definite tax savings. When a building is owned, only the depreciation on the cost of the building over its life can be charged off against taxes. But when everything is leased, the leasing charges are a straight expense deduction.
- Sale-leaseback can be used by both small and large businesses.
- This kind of financing can be used for the construction of new buildings as well as for already existing buildings.
- It may be possible to sell the building to a lessor at the depreciated value, eliminating the capital gains taxes.
- It is often possible to negotiate a renewal rate at some-

where between one third to one half of the original rate.

- It is also possible to purchase the building back at the end of the lease period at a preagreed price. But, if you are considering this maneuver, you should check carefully with a competent tax man.

GETTING BIG COMPANIES TO HELP YOU WITH EQUIPMENT AND SUPPLIES

The big companies that supply raw material to industry often find it very profitable to back a new venture with low-cost leasing deals on equipment. The equipment, of course, is to be used to process the raw materials they manufacture. This is a real insider's method, but one that anyone with a good idea can use. Just because you are not in business, or have had very little experience, is no reason to shy away from this technique. In fact, it is often the guy who takes charge of the situation who makes the best deal. After all, the big companies want to make more money, and if they are impressed with a person and his ideas, it is a small matter to back him with low-cost equipment lease back-up when he is planning to buy much of their raw materials to make his products.

Industries where you are most likely to be able to take advantage of this little-known but powerful method include chemicals, plastics, and sometimes foods. Douglas E. was a man who wanted to sell products through the mail, and he discovered that a fast profit could be made by producing certain chemical specialties packaged in aerosol cans. Doug was no chemist, but he knew the million-dollar secret of tapping the talents of others to make money. We are going to tell you his secret right now, so you can start your climb to wealth in a business of your own. Here it is:

THE MILLION-DOLLAR SECRET

Big chemical companies spend millions of dollars every year developing formulas for using the raw chemicals they produce. Most times, they use these formulas and raw chemicals to produce their own products. But, they will also offer many formulas—and even do custom formulation—for you at absolutely no charge. This may seem like an unusual gift, but when you consider that they want people to buy their raw chemicals, it is money well spent on their part. After all, if you start a business manufacturing products from their raw materials, they stand to prosper.

Here's the rest of Doug's story!

Doug went right to one of the biggest chemical manufacturers he knew and told them what he had in mind. Of course, he had carefully planned the details and rehearsed his proposal. He so impressed the people at this huge company that they not only gave him thousands of dollars worth of free formulas, they even put him in touch with four different companies that manufactured aerosol filling equipment. With recommendations like this, the equipment manufacturers were more than cooperative. In fact, three of them offered to lease their equipment at very favorable rates. Doug selected the best deal, set up in a rented two-car garage near his home, and soon found himself a chemical manufacturer even though he had only the vaguest idea of the chemical processes. His mail order business was aimed at industry, and today he is grossing close to a million dollars a year from a new plant.

MANY FRANCHISES ARE ACTUALLY LEASING DEALS

Many of the franchise companies are technically in the leasing business. Consider, for example, some of the ice cream operations. When you buy a franchise from them, you are actually leasing equipment from the people who produce the raw materials. Because you must have their materials to make ice cream, they arrange for the equipment lease at favorable rates in order to move their products. Of course, they do provide many other services, such as site selection and advertising. But, in its simplest form, this is a lease business where the lessor supplies the raw materials, and the lessee leases the equipment.

USING THE MODERN MAGIC OF SWAPPING SERVICES

The economics of the Middle Ages was essentially a barter system. People traded product for product and service for service. Of course, there can be little profit from such a system in the long run, but the technique is still very useful to modern businessmen, particularly those just starting out.

Let's suppose that you are planning to start a delivery service. You will need business cards, letterheads, envelopes, and perhaps some printed leaflets to advertise your service. Where would you go for these things? To a printer, of course. You could search out a smaller printer who either did not have his own delivery facilities, or one who handled his own deliveries with difficulty. When you found such a printer, it would be a small matter to trade your delivery services for his printing services. Of course, there is no cash profit in this, but after you have paid off the printer with a number of deliveries, the chances are very good that he will continue to use your services for pay. Naturally, you can operate this way with many other companies from whom you need services or products.

PROMISE A PIECE OF THE ACTION
TO GET WHAT YOU NEED

There are many people willing to speculate. Some of them will do it with money, and others will speculate with the talents and abilities they have. As a starting-out fortune builder, you can often attract very talented people to help you now for a promise of a reward later. This is done regularly in larger incorporated companies that sell stock to the public. When they sell stock, they are really promising a piece of the action to all the stockholders. You can do the same thing, even though you aren't incorporated and may be running a part-time business out of your basement. Here is the story of a man who turned a hobby into money, and built a successful operation with borrowed tools.

Carl J. worked for a cabinet maker, and was a first-rate craftsman. As a business, Carl decided to offer colonial reproductions. He would copy a piece of furniture someone had, or make a faithful reproduction from catalogs or decorator galleries. Of course, this kind of work required both skill and equipment. Fortunately, Carl found a man who ran a used tool exchange in a near-by town. When Carl told the dealer about his idea, the dealer offered to give, on long-term loan, the equipment he needed—all for "a piece of the action." Actually, the equipment had all been taken in on trade for new equipment, so the dealer was not really sticking out his neck very far. But as far as Carl was concerned, it was all he needed to put him into a very profitable business.

The two men drew up a simple contract and Carl was in business, without spending a cent on equipment. Because Carl's business was not a production operation, he was able to charge high prices for his furniture copies. As his reputation spread, Carl was able to buy new equipment for his expansion. Of course, the tool dealer still got all the business, and is still profiting from his foresight in giving Carl the machines he needed to get a start.

HOW TO MAKE THE MOST OF MANUFACTURERS' FREE TRIALS

You can get a trial run on many types of equipment normally used in business.

Let's say that you are interested in having several typewriters and a calculator for your office. First, visit several dealers and get demonstrations of the equipment you need. At this point, you will know which make of typewriter or calculator best suits your needs. Then, simply ask the dealer for a trial run. Dealers keep equipment for just this purpose, and will usually quickly install the machine you need for a month of free use. After a month, you may decide to buy or lease the machine, or even to return it. When you are planning to buy several machines, a month's free use can add up to quite a saving.

Don't try to play one dealer off against the other. We have heard of people who have done this with several dealers, taking each dealer's trial equipment for a month, and never buying from any of them. It's a small world, and word will get around. But, taking a month's free trial from the dealer from whom you plan to buy is fair play. After all, they do offer the service; but you should not abuse it.

CHECKLIST OF TECHNIQUES TO GIVE YOU THE EQUIPMENT AND TOOLS YOU NEED

- Get over the idea that you must own everything.
- When you lease property it is the same as borrowing the value of the property.

- Lease or buy? Let the tax advantages decide.
- Leasing can give you up-to-date equipment all the time.
- Leasing will free large amounts of capital for you to use in expanding your business.
- Use the sale-leaseback to get money quickly and save on taxes.
- Get big companies to help you with equipment and supplies.
- Learn how to swap services. Barter brings fast results.
- You can get tools and equipment today for a small piece of the action tomorrow.
- Be sure to make good use of manufacturers' free trials.

10

PYRAMID YOUR PROFITS WITH O.P.T. — OTHER PEOPLE'S TALENT

The chances are you are reading this book because you want to build something for yourself—either a part-time venture or a full-time business that will give you wealth and independence. In either case, you are probably a pretty independent person. You hesitate to ask for favors. You are the kind of person who has the spirit and drive to get things done and you like to do them by yourself. And, as such, you probably are reluctant to ask others for help when you need it. But, before you take on all of the problems yourself, let us tell you the story of a man who was fiercely independent, but who was able to use the best promotional brains in the country without charge or obligation.

Warren H. was a salesman for a large company. He was doing reasonably well, but he knew that if he was ever going to make it really big, it would not be through the ranks of the company that was giving him his bread and butter as a salesman. And, he knew that he was short on capital, but long on ideas. In fact, Warren did develop a commercial use for waste material that was thrown away daily by his employer.

Before he thought of going into business for himself, Warren had told his boss about the idea and all he got for his trouble was a laugh. Warren's boss had very little imagination, and he was not interested in having one of his subordinates come up with an idea that he should have developed himself. Warren immediately recognized that he was up against a stone wall. His boss would not give him the recognition he needed and there was no place to go in the company as long as he worked for this unreasonable man.

GETTING THOUSANDS OF DOLLARS WORTH OF PUBLICITY—FREE

Warren decided that he would try to start a part-time venture, with an eye to turning into a full-time business when the volume was sufficient. But, he didn't have the money to promote it nationally.

We told Warren that he could get his message to just about every industrial purchasing agent (his main market), without spending a cent for advertising, by preparing a simple photo of his product, an inexpensively printed news release, and sending it to the editors of many trade magazines. Warren did this, and within a few months, nine major industrial magazines carried small articles and pictures of his product. In six more months, Warren was so busy that he had to quit his selling job to devote more time to his rapidly expanding business. From an operation in his basement, he now has a plant with thousands of square feet, a home with a swimming pool in the country, and is planning to build a beautiful vacation home on a small island in the Caribbean. And he owes this to his rocket-fast start with OPT—Other People's Talent. In this case, it was the time and talent of the magazine editors that got him on the road to success and independence.

USING O.P.T. TO BUILD SUCCESS

No matter how many times you have run across people who will kick you when you are down, there are just as many people who will lend you a hand when you have ideas and the drive to see them through. The editors in the story we just told you were willing to do this, and because of them, Warren got thousands of dollars worth of free publicity for his idea. In fact, even now when Warren spends many thousands of dollars a year to advertise his greatly expanded line of products, he still leans heavily on the free publicity service offered by these helpful editors.

O.P.T., then is a commodity like money—other people's money. You can use it and you can profit from it. You can get it free, you can get it in exchange for services, you can get it on speculation, but the important fact is that you *can* get it and you must use it if you are starting with limited capital.

FINDING O.P.T. EVERYWHERE

Perhaps you are conjuring up the picture of a greedy person who will lend a hand only to collect heavily from you at some later date. People like this do exist, but believe us, there are more than enough people who have been through the mill who are ready and willing to give you the help you need, with no strings attached. For example, in New York City, there is a group of retired business professionals who help small businessmen every day. The Executive Volunteer Corps, as they are known, is made up of such people. You will be surprised just how helpful people can be when you ask. For one thing, people like to think that others are turning to them because of their achievement and stature. It means that they have arrived, that they are considered to be important people.

GETTING TOP EXECUTIVES TO GIVE YOU THE ANSWERS

We know of one man who regularly gets free, helpful advice from top corporation executives. He found that when he asked lesser management people for advice, they were often secretive and jealous of their information and position. But, when he asked the presidents of big companies, they were flattered by the request. Try it and you will see how easy it is to get to see top people. It's a lot more difficult to get to the lower managers, and they seldom have the answers.

HOW O.P.T. CAN MULTIPLY YOUR RESOURCES AND PROFITS

Consider for a minute a business that employs thousands of people. Such a business has every kind of specialist available on its staff, and these people are available to solve problems whenever they come up. But, you are starting a business that, for the time being, will employ no one but yourself. You will do everything, if you find the time—and have the experience. You will handle the bookkeeping ... the advertising ... the manufacturing ... the selling ... the office details ... and even carry out the garbage when the can is full. Discouraged? Don't be, because, if you follow our simple system, you can have all of these things done for you for little or no cost.

One of the big mistakes most small businessmen make is to try to be experts in every business operation. It can't be done, and unless you have the money to pay for these professionals, you will find yourself in trouble.

But, suppose you were able to find an accountant, an advertising man, an engineer, a salesman, and even an employment specialist—you would be able to tap Other People's Talent to build your business in half the time it would take alone. Consider just what it would cost to employ all of these people to do the work. And, imagine just what it would take to do all this work yourself. Is it any wonder so few new businesses survive?

As you should begin to see, by using Other People's Talent, you can virtually eliminate most of these problems, and you can get the kind of professional help that will assure your success.

HOW TO MAKE OTHER PEOPLE EAGER
TO WORK FOR YOU

You can stop making false starts on the path to wealth by carefully picking the brains of the professionals. It has been said that knowledge is power. No man can have all the knowledge needed to make a business a success. But, if he knows how to get other people to share their knowledge, this fact will be far more valuable than the combined skills of all the professionals helping him. And this is just what we are going to give you in the pages of this chapter.

"Why," you might ask, "would anyone be willing to help me?"

"I have very little money."

"I'm not sure that my idea will work."

"I have a limited education."

"There is a lot of competition."

And thousands of other excuses.

Regardless of how many reasons you can muster, it is still possible to get the help of talented professionals for little or no cost. Here are just a few of the things you can do to guarantee that other people will want to help you.

- *Have a solid idea.* This does not mean that the idea has to be completely original. After all, imagine how many hula hoops have been invented! But an old and successful idea, well thought out, is more likely to succeed than many dazzling, way-out schemes. For example, the simple idea of opening a store in an area where no stores like it exist has more chance of success than the once-in-a-million ideas that sometimes make the headlines. But, the idea must be sound, well researched, and carefully organized.

- *Have a positive mental attitude.* If you are going to attract other people to help you, you must be able to show them that you have confidence in your ideas. Often, the difference between success and failure when the same idea is tried by two different people is the attitude they project to other people. When a man has confidence in what he is doing, success is obvious to the people around him. When he is unsure, people are also aware of it, and are often unwilling to take a chance, or even to offer free advice. We have seen people with sound, but very ordinary ideas, turn them into wild successes only because they had the kind of an outlook that said to people, "This is a winner—this will succeed." People like to bet on winners. You must adopt a winner's outlook.

- *Be aware of what other people want.* When you seek the help, advice, and counsel of other people in your wealth-building activities, you must be aware of their own personal needs. For example, when you ask a person for advice, you are actually saying to him, "You, sir, are an expert and I am coming to you for help because I recognize your vast accomplishments." Of course, you would never use these actual words, but when you seek help from a person who has the background to offer the help, you are acknowledging his accomplishments. This makes the person feel important and he will do just about anything not to let you down. As we mentioned before, we know a man who has gotten much good advice and inside information from the heads of large corporations simply because he has a positive mental attitude and was aware of the fact that people of accomplishment like to maintain their image.

- *Dangle the carrot.* You may not be able to offer to pay for the accounting services you need. And, you may not be able to pay an advertising man to prepare a news release for you, but you can offer them future rewards without giving your business away. If you have carefully thought out your plans, you will have some idea of just where your venture will be in a year—or two years—and you can then tell these people that you will be able to offer them active and financially rewarding contracts then. For example, it is not uncommon for an accountant to offer his services to a prospective venture, if he believes in it, for the opportunity of handling the account when the business grows. You can, of course, do this with just about any of the other services you will need to start and operate your business. We will go into very specific detail on individual services you can tap later in this chapter. But, in the mean time, remember, the offer of a future reward for some early professional assistance can be a very powerful inducement for the help you will need.

TAPPING THE PRIME SOURCE OF O.P.T.

Before you go looking for outside talent to tap for your venture, be sure to check on the talent bank you inherited—your family. Many people are afraid to get involved with their family in a business way; but, properly handled, a family can often supply most of the talent needed to get a business off the ground.

We know many successful businesses that owe their success to the early employment of relative's talent. For example, Martin H. would never have made the success he did if it hadn't been for the fact that his brother had taken an accounting course in college. Mind you, his brother was not an accountant, but had only taken a few credits of accounting while majoring in economics.

Martin had started a small mail order business in his basement. He was selling office supplies and printed forms through the mail when his brother offered to take a look at the books. Martin was somewhat reluctant. First, because he was not anxious to let his brother know how he was doing; and second, because he thought that he was doing a good enough job by himself. After a review of the books and the botch that was made of the daily records, Martin's brother was able to put this business into the black quickly. Oddly enough, these brothers later joined forces in the business and today run one of the most successful mail order businesses we have ever seen.

You don't even have to rely on such sophisticated talent in your family. Consider the many husband-and-wife operations that make use of just about every member of the family. More often than not, the wife can type well enough to handle most of the correspondence. The kids can handle packing after school. And there are always enough relatives with the desire to earn a few dollars for part-time work. While this situation is ideal for starting a business, many husband-and-wife operations continue this way to make fortunes for an entire family.

DISCOVERING O.P.T. WITHIN WALKING DISTANCE OF YOUR HOME

Every neighborhood is a treasure trove of untapped talent. Housewives looking to earn a few extra dollars. Kids looking for after-school, part-time work. And even the men of the area hoping to pick up a few extra bucks for a Saturday job or do a few hours of work during the weekday evenings.

Whatever you need, the chances are that the talent exists within a few blocks of you right now. And, even if you cannot afford to pay these people for their efforts right now, if you are familiar with the ways to get other people eager to work for you, you will have more talent than you really need. After all, investing a little time and talent is often more rewarding than investing in the stock market. When you invest in stock, you gamble. But when you get a person to invest his time and talent, he has the feeling that he is, in a way, controlling the results of the entire project. People feel that they are part of something when they help.

In any neighborhood, there has to be an accountant, a secretary, an advertising man, an office manager, a printer, a shipping man, and just about every other talent you might need for your wealth-building ideas. Who could resist the promise of future rewards for a little part-time help? We know of many people who have added substantially to their income by offering such help to fledgling companies. We have heard of two teachers, one a teacher of commercial subjects and the other a manual arts instructor, who have gained a considerable interest in very successful businesses all because they were willing to spend a few hours a week helping a man long on ideas, but short on the experience these people had.

In fact, we know of one man, Robert W. who successfully assembled a group of people with the skills he needed by running a few classified ads in a local newspaper.

All he did was tell the truth. He stated that he was starting a business and needed help for which he could not pay—immediately. Not surprisingly, he was swamped with offers from people with every skill he needed. In fact, he even got the offer of additional seed capital from people who admired his very original approach. The people who did help him in his venture were ultimately given stock in his company, which is doing very well now, and is paying nice annual dividends to these far-sighted helpers.

USING ALL SOURCES OF O.P.T. TO BUILD WEALTH

How well do you really know your friends? Do you really know what they can do, other than what you have actually seen? For example, have you ever wondered what your co-workers might be able to do, other than the work for which they are now being paid?

You will be surprised at the amount of talent that lies below the surface of these people who you thought you really knew all along. Frank S. made his living as an engineer for many years. But, in his spare moments, he had dabbled with a simple silk screen printing press. He never told anyone about his interests and talents. But, one day, a friend of his, Harry G., mentioned that he had an idea for some decorative well hangings that could be produced by silk screen. Frank then told Harry about his press and his own interest in silk-screening and a very successful business venture was born immediately.

You don't even have to dig below the surface. Suppose that you are planning a home mail order business, but need help writing the sales messages. Perhaps the company you presently work for has an advertising manager who would welcome the opportunity to "moonlight" for you, writing the ads. Further, you might even be able to get professional help on the best way to handle the mailings and the shipping of the products from the shipping foreman of your company. Even the company bookkeeper might be interested in a part-time job for a piece of the action when the money starts to pour in.

Any social group, whether it is a lodge, church, profession, or trade club has many members who are often willing to donate their time and talent to help a friend get a business started. Don't be shy about asking. After all, it is the person with the positive mental attitude who attracts the help he needs. People like to be associated with a winner, and this attitude tells them that you will be a winner, and that they might be able to share in your future success.

HOW YOU CAN HAVE A MILLION-DOLLAR SALES FORCE FOR NO SALARY AT ALL

For the part-time business operator, unless he is in the mail order business, selling is usually the most difficult of the problems. We are now going to show you how you can have a million-dollar sales force without spending a penny in salaries

The secret lies in using manufacturers'
independent businessmen who sell for se
at a time and work strictly for commissio
make. These men confine their sales ac
narrow product lines. This means that th
quite hard for you. They strive to be very
own area of specialization.

Here's how they will work for you. They

you, and send the orders directly to you for shipment. You ship and bill the purchaser directly. Then, after you have been paid by the purchaser, you pay the commission to the agent. You retain all control over prices, terms, credit, and all the other conditions of sale. For this, however, most agents will expect that you give them exclusive rights to your products in their trading area. This is only fair, and doing so will make sure that your agents will work hard with your products.

Jeff. D. is a manufacturers' agent in Florida, handling swimming pool equipment. Many of the companies Jeff represents are large and well-known, but he also handles quite a few small operations that make a good profit for him and the company owners.

Jeff's customers aren't the swimming pool owners, but rather the pool builders and those offering maintenance service for pool owners. Among the larger products handled by Jeff is a line of pumps and expensive filter systems. But, in addition to these products, he handles a line of specialty chemicals for pool cleaning and water treatment which are produced by a one-man garage operation.

Jeff works on an average of 35 percent mark-up on these lines and travels the entire state for the companies he represents. But, he is always on the lookout for more lines. After all, when he makes a call on a pool contractor, it's just as easy to show ten products as it is to show five. But, the products must be related so that he can sell them to his existing customers as he travels the state. Jeff does very well for himself— and for the manufacturers he represents.

Now, here is an even more important advantage of using an agent. Each and every one of them is a well-spring of information—all of it free. When they are trying to sell your products, the people they call on will ask them about other products. If they get enough of these questions, they will tell you and suggest ways of making the products and getting them to market. This is a million dollars' worth of market research and it absolutely free.

Using a manufacturers' agent will give you these important advantages:

- *Economy.* It costs you nothing until a sale is made. You only pay a commission when the sale is made and the money has been collected from the customer. No high sales salary to worry about.
- *No run-away selling cost.* Because you will pay a commission only when a sale is made, you will never be stuck with high selling costs when sales are down. As sales go up so do your commissions, but you will never mind paying these costs. As sales costs go down, so will your selling costs. This is what always chokes a big company with a large sales force. In a slump, they still have to continue to pay their salaried salesmen. But, you will only pay for orders delivered.
- *Intense sales coverage.* Because most agents cover small segments of industry and geography, you will get intense coverage where you need it. You can pinpoint your important areas and get every cent of business from it.
- *Easy access to customers.* Because most agents carry several other related, but noncompetitive lines, you will get immediate access to the customers you want. These men are already covering the area, and when they take on your line, you will automatically have coverage that takes years for an individual company salesman to get.
- *High quality salesmanship.* More often than not, it is possible to get better sales coverage from an independent agent than from a salesman you might employ. Company salesmen, unless they are on a high commission basis, often become lazy when they reach a good income. However, the agent wants to keep your line, and will continue to sell hard for you.
- *Immediate sales.* When you tak[...] already calling on the people y[...] will have "instant sales." He doe[...] time developing the contacts. He [...] it is simply a matter of introduci[...] the people he already numbers as [...]

- *Automatic national sales offices.* Once you have set up a network of agents across the country, you literally have a series of national sales offices. And, of course, this is a lot easier, and less expensive to administer than a network of your own, salaried people in the same places.

Of course, there are disadvantages to using agents, but the advantages far outnumber them. There are two things to consider here. First, you seldom have any control over the way they sell. If you have developed any distinctive selling techniques, and your agent does not find them to his liking, he will not use them. But, as long as he gets the order, this can be a small matter. Second, because your agent will be carrying other lines, you will be getting only part-time coverage. But, remember that all of his lines must have something in common for him to make money. And, if he is calling on a company for one product, it is just as easy to pull yours out of the bag as well. In fact, it is for his benefit as well as yours.

HOW TO GET A NETWORK OF SALESMEN . . . FREE

You can locate the manufacturers' agents you want in several ways. Here are some of the success-tested methods we have suggested to others:

- Advertise in the business pages of newspapers in the area where you seek sales.

- Advertise in the business publications that reach the motivated sales people you want. For example, for only a few dollars, you can reach well over 10,000 active agents with a classified ad in *Agency Sales Magazine.* This is published by Manufacturers' Agents National Association, 3130 Wilshire Boulevard, Los Angeles, California 90010.

- You can often find people who might just be looking for your line by regularly reading such important business newsletters as *The Franklin Letter.* This newsletter contains a wealth of information for the small businessman. Available for $18 a year, it is published by the authors of this book; it is available from James

Franklin Associates, Box 95B, Demarest, New Jersey 07627.

- Call the agents listed in the Yellow Pages of the phone book. Remember this: if you are seeking agents in areas other than where you live, and you have a business phone, the phone company will supply you with out-of-town Yellow Pages without charge. And, if they happen to be out of the sections you want, you can always go to the phone company's regional office and use their own personal copies for reference.

SOLVING ALL OF YOUR EMPLOYMENT PROBLEMS ... WITHOUT CHARGE

Even if you start out with one person to help you—and that person is a part-time employee—you will need some assistance in the personnel area. And, of course, as you grow, so will your needs for professional personnel help. You can get top help—without spending a nickel. We're sure that you'd like to have someone:

- Determine the job requirements and locate the workers best qualified to do the work.
- Help you to keep the employees you have who are important to your growth.
- Plan personnel expansions and find the workers needed.
- Find and hire skilled workers in other parts of the country if there are none available in your area.
- Help you set up practical and easily-used personnel records and systems.
- Make use of free training programs for veterans.
- Help you to relocate your business in an area where there is an ample supply of workers and desirable community facilities.

Yes, it is possible to have all these things—and more—done for you absolutely free. All you have to do is contact the local office of the United States Employment Service, describe your problems and requirements, and they will get the job done for you without charge. In fact, if you would like to know about all of the services you can tap free, write to the United States Employment Service, Bureau of Employment Security, U.S. Department of Labor, Washington, D.C. and ask for a copy of the publications of the U.S. Employment Service. This informative bulletin lists, describes, and explains how to order all Employment Service Bulletins which are available.

If you would like to receive monthly information on employment conditions in any state, simply write to the State Department of Labor in a particular state and ask them to put you on the list for their regular and free bulletins. There is a wealth of material in each of these monthly publications.

Remember this: when you use their services, you, and only you are the final judge when it comes to hiring. But the Employment Service will pull out all the stops to find, test, and screen the people for you to make your personal choice. We feel that this is one of the best bargains available to the small businessman from the Federal Government. And, the price is right. It's free.

A MILLION DOLLARS WORTH OF FREE ADVERTISING CAN BE YOURS FOR THE ASKING

As we mentioned earlier, it is possible to get the editors of most national magazines to run news releases and short articles on your new product or service by simply sending them a page of copy and a photo. This is part of their job, and they are always on the lookout for something new that will be of interest and benefit to their readers. But, suppose that you find it simply impossible to write this news release yourself and do not know where, or who, to send the releases to. The answer is simple. Use advertising O.P.T.

Ed C. had an idea for selling bird house kits by mail, but he was short on money. Ed thought that he might get the help of an advertising agency, but was staggered by the costs involved. However, the president of the agency thought that Ed had a good idea and he offered to do a news release and send it to all of the publications reaching people who would be interested in bird houses. The agency president did this without charge, but he did get Ed to agree to use his agency when and if the business became successful. About half a dozen magazines picked up the story and Ed was in business overnight. And, the agency president who had supplied the O.P.T. had acquired a client for life.

A well-planned and carefully written release can cost anywhere from $150 to $500. But, many an agency has found it to be quite profitable to do a release on "speculation" for a person who lacked money, but had good ideas. Be sure to look for a smaller agency to help you. The larger agencies are often overworked and are seldom interested in betting on the future of someone else's ideas.

Of course, when the release is prepared it will be sent to the editors of all the magazines that would be of value to you, and the editors then do their O.P.T. thing for you by running the item in their columns. The rest is up to you when the inquiries and orders flood you out of your basement workshop and send you rocketing up the ladder of business success.

HOW NEWSPAPER EDITORS CAN MAKE YOU RICH

If your business or service is to be offered strictly on a local basis, you can pull the same approach with a local newspaper editor. After all, he is interested in news, and a new business (which might become a future advertiser) is always welcomed for an editorial mention. As a matter of fact, you can use the approach we described before with an advertising agency executive. He will, more than likely, be willing to lend a hand on a speculative basis. And, his connections with the local papers will be much stronger than yours are presently. Put the two together, and you have actually multiplied the power of Other People's Talent.

TAPPING THE O.P.T. OF EDUCATIONAL PROFESSIONALS

College and university professors are seldom overpaid. For this reason, many of them "moonlight" in their area of specialty. Most colleges have business departments, engineering departments, and other professionals available to lend an O.P.T. hand.

When Tom B. thought about starting a business of his own, he was immediately discouraged by both his lack of business experience and his limited funds. But, Tom was a good cook, and many people knew this. In fact, he used to "moonlight" from his drafting job to run cook-outs for local organizations. At one of his moonlighting cook-outs, Tom began chatting with a guest and told him of his one desire to do the thing he liked best—cooking.

It turned out that the man he was speaking with was a professor of business at a near-by college. The professor liked Tom—and his cooking—and offered to help him for a piece of the action, actually only 5 percent of the profits.

The professor, at his own expense, conducted a survey of the roads in town, and the eating habits of both the local residents and those just passing through. After spending considerable time, he was able to come up with a location and a restaurant idea that tapped both sources of customers. He was also able to use his business consulting influence to swing a loan with a local banker for the money needed to start the restaurant.

Within a very short time, Tom was in business, and the professor not only had a percentage of the profits, he had also found a place to eat with a man who could outcook anyone else in town. Tom is now pocketing over $25,000 each year, and the professor has added about $1,200 a year to his income —for life.

Again, it is the lure of sharing in a success that will enable you to get these people to lend you their talent. The authors of this book personally know several people who have gotten what is normally very expensive consulting services from university faculty members for only a few shares of stock, or a promise of payment if the venture succeeds.

You will be surprised how receptive these professionals will be to a well-conceived idea that can make money. Here are just some of the faculty people who can be of help and what they might be able to do for you:

- *Professors of accounting.* They can not only help you to set up a bookkeeping system, they can counsel you on all the financial aspects of starting and running a business.
- *Marketing and advertising professors.* They can guide you in your selling, advertising, and marketing.

- *Other business professors.* You can get aid on personnel, administration, management, and just about every other aspect of business administration.
- *Professors of engineering.* If you need help with product design or manufacture, these are the people to call on. We know of one company who developed a complete line of industrial products by using the chairman of the engineering department from a local college. They both profited very handsomely, but the company did not have the problem of paying a high-priced man during the stage when the products were being developed and there were no sales.
- *Psychologists.* These men can be very helpful in handling personnel problems, as well as counseling on management and market research problems. Many can offer sound guidance on problems of consumer behavior which will relate to both product design and advertising.
- *Economists.* Although economists tend to be more theoretical than other people, it is often possible to find one with his feet on the ground who can offer sound advice on short- and long-range business planning, as well as financial matters.
- *Special areas.* If, for example, you are planning to do something in the art field, you can draw upon such talent in a college art department. The same for music. In fact, there is hardly an area of commerce where you will not be able to find a college faculty member with some expertise who would be willing to lend you his personal O.P.T.

HOW TO MAKE OTHER PROFESSIONAL PEOPLE— BANKERS, LAWYERS, AND ACCOUNTANTS— ANXIOUS TO FURTHER YOUR SUCCESS

Lawyers and accountants have two things to sell—time and talent. When you buy from them, they do not take a product off the shelf. They make their money giving you advice—advice that is based on many years of schooling and professional work. Therefore, when you seek the O.P.T. of these people, it is wise to approach them with this thought in mind. Here, you should emphasize that their help is actually an investment, much the same as it would be if they were to take thousands of dollars and place it in the stock market. But, you can play a trump card. When a man invests in the stock market, unless he is spending millions, he has absolutely no control over the company in which he is investing.

But, when he invests himself, by giving you the help you need, he will have a personal control over the possibility of future gain. The better he does his job of advising you, the better are his chances of making money when your enterprise makes it big.

For example, many lawyers we know and have heard of have made fortunes, not in the courtrooms, but in the board rooms of the corporations they helped when they were just starting. The same holds true for accountants and even for bankers, where financial advice was the service offered.

When Ralph D., an attorney, was completing the work necessary to set up a corporation for Claude R., he found that Claude had some very interesting ideas about how to make money servicing electronic equipment for local factories.

"How much money do you figure it would take to set up a business just to do this service work?" Ralph asked Claude at one of their meetings.

Claude's original purpose in setting up a company was to do TV service work, and he really hadn't thought much about how much money it would take to start this kind of a business. But, he said, "$10,000 should be enough."

Before Claude left Ralph's office that day, the two had concluded a deal whereby Ralph would put up the $10,000 and throw in the legal services for only one third of the business. Now, instead of a simple TV repair business, Claude is in a big-time electronics repair business. His lawyer had sensed a way to make money, had given Claude the money and the legal help he needed, and a new business was born. Actually, Ralph had also gotten an accountant to do the books for only ten shares of corporate stock.

Last year, Claude had pocketed about $35,000, or about

$15,000 more than he had expected to make when he sat down with Ralph to do the legal work on his original idea, a TV repair shop.

CHECKLIST FOR PYRAMIDING YOUR PROFITS WITH O.P.T.

- O.P.T. is a commodity just like money. You can get it free, you can get it in exchange for services and you get it on speculations . . . but you *can* get it.
- Get the help of top corporate officers simply by asking.
- Multiply your resources by using the talents of others.
- Make others eager to help you with their O.P.T. Have a solid idea. Have a positive mental attitude. Be aware of what other people want. Dangle the carrot.
- Be sure to make use of the talent you inherited—your family.
- Bring in your talented neighbors, co-workers, friends, and business associates.
- Use manufacturers' agents for a million-dollar sales force without a payroll.
- Use the United States Employment Service to solve your personnel problems professionally and without charge.
- Get millions of dollars worth of free publicity with a simple news release.
- Tap the talent of college faculty members.
- Other professionals, bankers, lawyers, and accountants will lend a hand.

11

HOW TO ACQUIRE
A BUSINESS WITH LITTLE
OR NO CASH INVESTMENT

When we tell people who want to build fast personal wealth that it is possible to acquire a going, profitable business without a penny of cash investment they scoff. But, people just like you are doing it every day, and with the information we are about to give, *you* will be able to do it, too. To put this powerful technique into its proper focus, let us tell you the story of Bob T., a man who also scoffed at the idea of owning a business for no cash investment, but who has done it very successfully.

Bob was a hard worker who sold advertising space for a large publisher. It was his job to call on advertisers and advertising agencies five days a week to try to sell them advertising in the pages of his employer's magazines. Most of Bob's time was spent with advertising agencies and, early in his selling career, Bob decided that he wanted to be in the advertising agency business for himself. He had the sales experience, knew enough about advertising to do the job, had the guts, but simply didn't have the money needed to get going. Like so many people who dream of wealth, Bob plugged away at his selling job, but he did try to set away some money for the day when he would make the break and start his own advertising agency.

After several years of hard work and dreaming, Bob sat down to take stock of his money and his ambitions. To his sorrow, he found that he had been able to save only $2,350 in five years—hardly enough to start a business, and never enough to keep it going until it became profitable. Naturally, Bob was downhearted, and he mentioned his seemingly shattered dreams to Charles L., the president of a small advertising agency he had called on one day. Mr. L., normally a harried, and short-tempered man, sat quietly and listened patiently to Bob's sad tale. After Bob had finished, the man abruptly suggested they have dinner that evening at his club. Naturally, Bob was surprised, but he quickly accepted the offer, not really knowing what the other man had in mind.

At dinner that evening, Mr. L. told Bob that he had been planning to retire, and offered to sell Bob the agency. Naturally, Bob was elated and he was anxious to take over this small, but very successful business. In fact, the price seemed more than fair. Mr. L. quoted it at twice annual earnings, which is a traditional approach for selling most types of businesses. Bob was all but ready to spend his savings, plus several thousand dollars he managed to scrape up from relatives, until he talked to us. We told him the important secret of acquiring such a business for *no money at all.*

HOW TO GET A BUSINESS FOR NO CASH INVESTMENT

Charles L.'s agency, the business Bob was planning to buy, is considered a *service* business. That is, it has no products that can be pulled off the shelf and sold to customers. It's strength lies in the services performed by Charles L., the owner, and his employees, not in any products to be sold. This is absolutely the most risky kind of a business to buy *for cash,* but it is also the easiest kind of a business to acquire with *no cash investment.* After all, what is *really* owned by such a business? Typewriters, desks, office machines, and that's about it.

These are all things anyone can buy from an office supply business, and if you were to price the physical assets, they would only come to a fraction of the price Charles L. is placing on the business.

But ... Mr. L. will glibly tell you that he has many clients who spend thousands of dollars every year with him. Here's the key—they spend it with *him*. As far as the customers are concerned, Charles L. *is* the business, and he is supplying services only to his customers. The customers will have no idea of whether or not a new owner can supply the same services as they have been used to getting. After all, in any kind of a service business there are strong personal preferences and loyalties, and they are all based on the performance of one or a few individuals in the business. If these individuals were to leave or sell out, there just may be no business at all. And this is just what happens to many types of service businesses when they are sold.

So, when Bob came to us with his apparent good fortune, we had to advise him against spending his money. But, we did tell him that he could acquire this business without spending his own or borrowed money. Bob was able to convince Charles L. that the chances would be great that he would make more under our plan than he would by trying to sell outright for cash. Here's the way the plan works:

- Bob was made a "partner" in the business. That is, Charles L. actually hired him, with a salary, to work for the agency.

- With Bob as a "member of the firm," Charles L. wasted no time in introducing him to all of his clients. In a very short time, Bob had taken over the servicing of the clients—but under the background guidance of the owner, Mr. L.

- As Bob's experience and confidence grew and as the clients grew accustomed to him, rather than to Charles L., Bob came to symbolize the business.

- Once most of the clients were satisfied with the new "partner," Charles L. announced his retirement, but added that he would remain with the business in an advisory capacity. This, of course, was to further soften the transition for both Bob and the customers.

- Bob was now the proud owner of his own very successful advertising business without spending a nickel of his own money.

HERE'S HOW TO "FINANCE" A FREE BUSINESS

- First, note that Bob did not pay Charles L. a penny in cash to acquire the business outright.

- Bob made an agreement with the owner to pay him for the business out of profits over a five-year period. He paid either a fixed amount, or a percentage of profits, whichever was greater, each year.

- Because the business was already making money, this was easy. And, as it turned out, Charles L. finally got more than he had been asking for when he was trying to sell it outright for cash. Because Charles was planning to retire, he had somewhat neglected the business for a while, so profits were not as good as they were when he had first started. And, because Bob was anxious for the really big money, he went out and hustled a lot of new and very profitable business. This really ran up the profits and Charles L. was pleasantly surprised at the end of each of the five years. Of course, Bob didn't mind paying this out because he, too, was making much more money than he had ever made as an employee, and even more than he had dreamed he could in his own business.

GETTING A SERVICE BUSINESS WITH NO CASH INVESTMENT

Use your imagination and you will see that there are many other types of service businesses that have very little physical worth because of the reasons we have just mentioned. The owners of such businesses will try very hard to convince you that the "good will" of the business is what you are buying, but unless you can stitch up an agreement as we have just described, be very careful about buying such a business for cash.

USING THE 1-2-3 FORMULA TO ACQUIRE A BUSINESS WITH NO CASH INVESTMENT

Look around you and see just who is making the really big money. For the most part, the people who are in business for themselves who are really making it are in services. They are building fast personal and business fortunes without ever handling a product or being stuck with heavy inventory. It is true—about half of the money produced in this country today is the result of services. And, remember this—services are expanding more rapidly than any other kind of business. This means that your chances of acquiring a business by the methods we are describing are getting better all the time. And, to simplify your task, we have developed our simplified 1-2-3 formula for acquiring a business with no cash investment. But, before you begin your program of business acquisition, you must carefully consider these important characteristics:

- the business must be a service business
- the business must have a minimum of assets, equipment, and stock
- it should have little or no long-term debt
- the owner should be looking for a way out
- and the owner must be willing to work with you before his customers are notified of the transfer

All of these conditions make it ripe for you to move in with a solid proposal and to take over the business without a nickel of investment capital. Here's the 1-2-3 formula:

1. Before you ever start looking at actual businesses, take stock of yourself. Ask yourself what you like to do, and what you would like to be doing for the rest of your life. It is important in any business that you like what you are doing. Nothing could be worse than to work in a business of your own that you do not like. After all, millions of people now work for others, hating every minute of it. If you are planning to make money in a business of your own, be very sure that you will be happy in your work. You now have the opportunity to pick and choose—so do it very carefully.

Here are just a few examples of service-oriented businesses you might consider: employment agency, real estate agency, floor waxing and other home service type businesses, sewer cleaning, painting contractor, manufacturers' representative, messenger service, locksmith, lawn maintenance and landscaping, janitorial services, detective bureau, catering business, guard and protection service, auctioneering, and so on. As you can see from this very brief sampling, there are many different kinds of service businesses that you can pick up and develop without spending a nickel to buy.

2. Once you have a feel for the kind of a business you would like, then you should actively seek out the names and addresses of every one within commuting distance of your home. Then write, asking if they might be interested in retiring from their business. Be careful not to mention that you are interested in "buying." This can be implied when you write, but the words "buy" and "sell" should be carefully avoided. There is nothing wrong about doing this. Business brokers do it every day. It is the best way they have to develop leads for businesses that they can sell to others for a commission. Once you start getting replies, be quick to follow them up. You should visit every one who responds and be very frank about what you have in mind.

Don B. wanted to buy an employment agency and he wrote to a half dozen in his area, as we suggested. He got three responses and quickly phoned each agency owner to set up an appointment.

Being frank and direct is important in this kind of negotiation. "I want to buy your business," Don told each owner, "but I simply do not have a lot of cash—and I know how hard it would be for you to sell a personal service business."

Because each of the owners had not seriously considered selling until they had heard from Don, the advantage was on Don's side. Don said to each: "You will have a good income from your business for quite a while, and you may even end up making more from it than you are now making. After all, it is very difficult to sell a personal service business for a lump-sum price and I am willing to work to build up the business and to pay you a share of the profits for a long period of time." Don pointed out that this would be like having an annuity and it had a great appeal to two of the three owners.

Actually, Don acquired one of the businesses on this basis, and six months later one of the other owners called back to re-open negotiations. Don then took on the second operation, which was in another city, as a *branch* of his now fast-growing employment agency. With a personal income of $40,000 per year, Don was quite happy with his no-cash acquisitions. And so were the people who had sold their businesses to him.

You must be sure to get an agreement from the owner that he will not open a competitive business after he agrees to have you take over the present operation.

3. Once you come to terms, you should then begin working in the business as quickly as possible. The customers should not be told of the plan, only that you are working for the company, and that you will be working closely with them in the future. Then, as they accept you, and it becomes apparent that there will be no loss of business, you should arrange with the previous owner that he will remain to smooth the transition. He should then announce to the customers that he will serve the business on a consulting basis, insuring that the customers will continue to get the best possible service, and assuring that they will continue to buy from you, the new owner.

You will then be the owner of a business in which you have invested nothing. But, you will be investing yourself, the most precious commodity you own. Just because you now own a going business, don't slack off. Now is the time to dig in and build it up to the kind of business that will allow you to realize your dreams of wealth and independence, and possibly pass it on to someone else in a few years for your share of the "annuity."

START OR BUY—YOUR MOST IMPORTANT DECISION

We have just showed you how to acquire a business without investing a cent. But, this approach is most workable with service types of businesses. You may want to get into a retail business, or any other type of business that involves expenses either in equipment or inventory. If this is your meat, you must then decide whether you want to start one from scratch or try to buy a business that is already "going." There are many advantages to both, but let's take a look at the advantages of buying a "going" business:

BUYING A GOING BUSINESS—LOOK FOR THESE ADVANTAGES:

- It is often possible to buy a going business for a bargain price. Many times people decide to move to another part of the country for one reason or another, and find it impossible to take the business with them. When this occurs, you can often pick up a going money-maker for very little money. Business brokers can often put you in touch with people in this situation. They are usually called in after the owner has been unsuccessful in selling the business by himself. He is then willing to pay the commission to the broker to get the business off of his hands in a hurry.

- When you buy a going business, you will save a lot of time and effort. If the business is successful, it will have established clientele, stock, and equipment. This can be invaluable when you are in a hurry to make the really big money.

- You will be able to benefit from the successes and mistakes of the present owner. After all, everyone makes mistakes, and if the owner can tell you what he did wrong as well as what he did right, you will be way ahead of the game.

AVOIDING SOME OF THE PITFALLS

- Be sure to investigate very carefully before you decide to take over someone else's business. On the surface, many proposals sound like you will make a million overnight. Most businesses offered for sale are sound, but many of them are offered at inflated prices. This means that they are still worth buying, but that the sale price should be carefully evaluated. Some will have minor problems, but this does not mean that they should not be considered. However, they should be considered at a lesser price than the seller is asking. You might even consider getting an outsider's opinion, and here is a good place to practice the art of O.P.T. Your accountant and attorney just might be willing to make the appraisal for a piece of the action, as we described in the last chapter.

- Check the reputation of the owner very carefully. There are two types of reputation a businessman can have; one is the reputation he has with his customers and the other is his standing with his suppliers. Check both very carefully. It is important to know if the people who supply the business will continue to work with you after you have taken over. If there is a problem with supplier credit, don't hesitate to trade on Other People's Credit. You can often get people with good credit, as we described before, to lend their name to your enterprise to bolster the credit rating.

- Check the location very carefully. Be careful that you are not buying a business that is dying because the location is out of step with business. For example, many diners and restaurants that have been very successful have "gone under" because of a change in a highway location that previously brought most of the business. These changes may not be readily apparent, so be sure to check to see if the zoning regulations have been changed and if these changes will effect the future success of the business.

- Make sure that the actual assets of the business are up-to-date and in good condition. If the previous owner has had the same fixtures for years, they may be outdated and in need of repair. This can be an added expense before you even get started. Depending on the type of business, you might be able to trade some of your services for new equipment, as we described earlier.

- Check the inventory carefully. The previous owner may have bought and stocked unwisely. For example, if you are buying a clothing shop and it is Fall, be wary of a heavy inventory of summer clothing. The styles for summer clothing will probably change dramatically by next year and the stock you take over may be worthless. If you have no way of getting rid of this stock, you must make the previous owner discount it from the price of the business.

HOW TO BUY A PROFITABLE BUSINESS

Make sure that the business you are considering is making or can make a profit. Make sure that it has been profitable over the years it has been going. Watch for anything unusual. For example, if a business has shown regular profits over the years, and suddenly shows either a huge profit or loss for a single year, watch out. You must see all the financial records for the years in which the business has been operating. If the owner is hesitant about showing them or claims that they have been lost, remind him that the tax records are available, and that they will tell the story you want.

LOOK FOR A HIGH RATE OF RETURN

You must have something to compare when you plan to buy a business. Compare the amount you plan to invest in the business with what you might be able to get with another business investment. Check the returns for the past five years and see if they compare favorably with what you have made over the same period. And, most importantly, how does the return compare with other businesses in the same field? It is possible to get comparable figures for the business that interests you from the Federal Government, and we will show you in a later chapter where to go to get this information.

BUYING A BUSINESS WITH HIGH EXPENSES

Don't hesitate to consider a business that has had a low profit. It just might be low because the present owner has not been realistic about his expenses. With other things being equal, such a business is often a very good buy. If the business is sound, and you can see a way to trim the expenses, it is a good sign that you will make it a profitable business.

Of course, as the business grows, you should avoid the temptation to add needless expenses. But, this doesn't mean that you shouldn't reward yourself with a few of the pleasures of ownership. A company-owned car is a deductible business expense, whether it is a Cadillac or a Ford, but it often costs you less in the long run if the business owns it, rather than if you buy it yourself out of your salary. If you want a bigger car, and the business can afford it, don't hesitate to treat yourself well. But, remember there are many ways of rewarding yourself and, depending on your tax bracket and the business structure, you should investigate all avenues.

Be sure to get your O.P.T. accountant to set up the best deal for you.

BUYING A BUSINESS THAT WILL GROW

When you consider buying a business, the only thing you will have to review will be its past history. But, with good records, you should be able to tell where the business has been and where it will go with the same expenditure of money and effort. And, it is quite easy to predict where the business will go with the changes you plan, based on your evaluation of the business history.

Lois M. bought a dry goods business with a good history and good prospects. Her O.P.T. accountant, Roger W., went over the history with her and informed her that by turning the profits back into the company for one year, she would be able to expand the business well beyond its present rather successful situation. The profits for a year averaged about $8,000. Lois actually borrowed this much money (through a banker friend using the O.P.T. methods we have described) and acquired the store next door. With her doubled space and increased newspaper advertising, Lois was able to turn an already successful business into a raging success.

After the first year, she had returned the borrowed $8,000, turned an additional $7,000 profit, and paid herself a salary of $17,000. Five years later, Lois had managed to acquire two other stores in other cities, and has made herself a cool $50,000 each year.

STAYING OUT OF OTHER PEOPLE'S DEBTS

Watch out for a heavily mortgaged business. Make sure that the owner has not contracted for supplies which have not yet been delivered—and billed. The bills will appear just as soon as you take over. Of course, there are always current liabilities in any business, but these will appear in the financial statement and should be deducted from the agreed-upon value of the assets to determine what you will actually pay for the business.

GETTING MAGIC MONEY WITH THE MINI-MERGER

Once you have your business firmly established, the chances are that you will want to grow and expand. Of course, the best way is to make the present business grow by selling harder, advertising more, and adding services or products to the line. But, it is also possible to grow by adding companies just the way you would add products to your line.

If you acquired your business by the methods we have just described, it will now be even easier to acquire other companies by the same methods. At this point, you will have a company with history, and retirement-interested owners will be even more intrigued by your proposals of mergers. Actually, the word merger is reserved for public corporations—companies with stock sold to the public. But, even if you are a sole proprietor or a partnership, and are not incorporated, you can use the money-making tactics of the merger. We have called this powerful method the "Mini-Merger."

Rather than trade stock, and get involved with all of the details necessary for corporations to merge, you can use the ease and simplicity of your small business to grow at a fantastic rate by simply acquiring other businesses with the Mini-Merger technique. And, it is not necessary to look for businesses similar to your own. In fact, it is often very advantageous to seek out other types of businesses to broaden your base of operations. But, remember, you must seek out service types of businesses and apply the same methods we have already described to get you into business. The advantage you now have is that you can show the owners of businesses you would like to acquire a sound financial picture and give them a plan for a pay-out that they know will make them a lot of money when you take over the business.

In fact, it is also possible to accelerate your growth by an even greater rate by seeking businesses and keeping the owner as a manager. Quite often it is possible to find a business that has been marginally successful for one reason or another. If the owner knows his business, but has been hindered by lack of capital, you can propose a business "marriage" in which you acquire the business, and the owner is retained on a salary to run it for you. You can then bring to the business the experience and money it needs, along with the effort of the previous owner, to make it a real winner. There have been many one-man businesses that have lumped along for years until they joined forces with another one-man business in a Mini-Merger to produce very profitable enterprises. Of course, remember that you must come out on top. When you acquire such a business, it becomes your business and the former owner is now your employee. But, you must offer some incentive, other than a salary, if the former owner is going to be the asset you need. Bonuses based on profits are the best way to handle this.

Paul W. saw the "Mini-Merger" as a way to expand his small, but successful home service business. Paul had been sort of a handyman, doing work like storm window installation, some landscaping, and floor waxing and surfacing. He had worked hard, and he had been fairly well rewarded for his efforts. But, he could not grow because he had just enough personal time to handle the work he already had for his business. And, he wasn't too anxious to add the expense of employees.

Paul knew a man, Jim L., who had a window cleaning business and who was in the same boat. With the "Mini-Merger" in mind, Paul proposed the business "marriage" with the agreement that Jim remain in the combined business. Jim liked the idea and sold out to Paul for $4,000. But, remember, Jim stayed on and the profit capacity was greatly increased for both of them. They could save considerable time as well. When Jim had a floor job and Paul had a window job at the same house, only one man would go and handle the work. The saving in time and money is a very important part of the Mini-Merger.

Later, Paul also acquired a complete landscaping service as well as a furniture cleaning business. Through the use of the Mini-Merger Paul had actually built himself a small conglomerate of service businesses. As the head of his own company, Paul became accustomed to earning well over $30,000 each year. And, each of the people he acquired with his Mini-Mergers actually made more money working for Paul than they would have if they had stayed on their own.

HOW INSIDERS USE THE CORPORATE SHELL

The merger route can be traveled by anyone who knows the "shell game." Suppose you want to acquire a small company, but have only limited funds. And, suppose that you are not even incorporated. Here's how the insiders handle this bit of money magic.

Martin W. was a man of very modest means, but he saw an opportunity to acquire a small, only slightly profitable company. In fact, the owners of the company had been looking for the chance to sell for quite a while. Martin had a few dollars, but he simply did not have the amount needed to swing the deal. Instead, Martin bought a corporate "shell." This is a legal corporation, but one which has very little value. The one Martin bought had manufactured dental supplies, and had fallen on hard times. The assets of the corporation had been sold, and the stockholders had been paid their money from the sale. The stock was still owned by the shareholders, and the corporation was still in legal existence, but the whole thing was next to worthless.

HOW TO BECOME THE OWNER OF A CORPORATION FOR VERY LITTLE MONEY

Martin, through a business broker, arranged for and bought the corporate shell for less than $10,000. He was now the owner of a corporation with stockholders and a fair amount of un-issued stock. With this stock in hand, Martin approached the company he really wanted to buy and offered to acquire it for some of the stock in his newly acquired corporation. Because the owners were tired of the operation, it looked like a good deal to them and they sold. After all, it might be possible for them to make more money on the stock of this company, of which their company was now part, rather than to continue pushing their own stock themselves.

Once Martin bought the company, he was able to liquidate a lot of the inventory and supplies and convert them into ready cash. His next step was to call a directors' meeting and authorize the issuance of convertible securities and use the proceeds to handle his next acquisition. Martin is still buying and is a very wealthy man because he played the corporate shell game —a perfectly legal way of making money. Martin did with $10,000 what might have cost $50,000 or more if he had not gone the corporate shell route.

DON'T BUY A BUSINESS—JUST RENT THE CUSTOMERS

Without customers you do not have a business. Regardless of what business you choose, if you do not have anyone to sell to, you cannot make money. Suppose we told you that you could make money from your kitchen table, working only a few hours a week and using someone else's customers to make you rich? You'd either think we were crazy or about to tell you something illegal. We are neither, and you can do this with very little money—and you can do it from any place in the world. It's called the mail order business and it is one of the easiest businesses in which to make a fortune.

When you go into the mail order business, you will have products to sell and you will try to sell them to specific markets. For example, if you are trying to sell cookbooks through the mail, you certainly would not have many truck drivers buying your books. What we are saying is this—you can rent lists of people with just about any characteristic you want. And, you can be sure that they are people who will be interested in and ready to buy your products. The best way to get information on these lists is to contact the Direct Mail Advertising Association, Inc., at 230 Park Avenue, New York, New York 10017. They will be happy to put you in touch with mailing list brokers who will be able to get you just about any list you want.

Mail order seems to be the dream of most people who consider a home type of business. Even though there is much money to be made in such a business, it still requires some work. When Carol W. decided to make money with her hobby, needlepoint, she thought that mail order would be the best way to go about it. She designed a number of patterns, stenciled them on canvas backing and had instructions printed for the hobbyist to use in "creating" a finished piece.

To get started, Carol rented the mailing list belonging to a publisher of craft magazines, and soon had built herself a nice little home mail order business. Later, she tried other lists, and after careful testing found that she could use the same list three or four times each year and still get the same return— about 2 percent. This may not seem like a lot, but if your costs are in line, and you make your mailings consistantly, it is possible to make quite a bit of money with someone else's customers. Carol's part-time mail order venture brought her $9,000 a year. Not bad for a "Saturday-only" operation.

If you are seriously considering the mail order business, one of the best sources of current and up-to-date information is *The Franklin Letter*.

HOW TO FIND THOUSANDS OF
AVAILABLE BUSINESSES

Every Sunday, *The New York Times* and most major metropolitan newspapers run ads for hundreds of businesses for sale. On a daily basis, *The Wall Street Journal* does the same thing. And, the monthly *Franklin Letter* also lists and describes many profitable business opportunities in each issue. You should begin reading these publications very carefully and you will soon see that the business you want is available and for sale.

You should also check with business brokers for their current listings. These people can be a big help because they often know of specific businesses available that have not been advertised to the general public. These brokers can be found in the Yellow Pages of your local telephone directory.

Another good way to find out about businesses for sale is by contacting commercial real estate people. They often act as business brokers, and those who do not often have information on available businesses for sale resulting from their real estate dealings.

CHECKLIST OF LOW-CASH BUSINESS ACQUISITION TECHNIQUES

1. Decide, first, on a service type of business to use the "no-cash" method of acquiring a business.

2. Make a firm proposal to the owners of these service businesses to acquire their operations and pay them out of profits. Remember, service businesses have very little in terms of capital assets, and they are easily acquired because of this.

3. Use the 1-2-3 formula for acquiring a business with no cash investment.

4. Decide whether you want to start or buy a business. Compare the costs of doing both before you decide.

5. Buy a profitable business—one that can be shown to be on the way to making profits.

6. Look for a high rate of return.

7. Buy a business with low expenses. You may be able to buy a less profitable business, and turn it to profits by trimming expenses.

8. Buy a business that can grow.

9. Watch out for other people's debts.

10. Try the "Mini-Merger" method to expand rapidly and profitably.

11. The corporate shell is the way to play the merger game.

12. Read all of the publications that advertise business opportunities regularly.

12

HOW YOU CAN TURN THE POWER OF TIME AND SPACE INTO A PERSONAL FORTUNE

"Time is money" is an old saying, but for today's wealth-seeker it has a different and powerful meaning. Radio and television advertising is referred to as time. In fact, those people who work for the stations to sell advertising are referred to as time salesmen.

When you hear the astronomical prices paid for a few seconds of time on a radio or television show, the chances are that you have never even considered using either to promote your product or service. But we are going to give you, for the first time in a book of this kind, the insider's secret of harnessing this time as well as the space sold in publications for advertising. And, the miracle of this secret is that you will not have to spend a cent to get your product before millions of people who want to buy. Earlier in this book, we discussed the methods of getting publicity in publications. This is a good start, but now we will show you how to get your product right on the *paid* advertising pages of publications, announced on the radio along with other paid announcements, and placed on television shows where the cost per minute often runs many thousands of dollars—*all free.*

USING THE P/I FORMULA TO REACH MILLIONS OF PEOPLE

In discussing this method, we are going to introduce you to several powerful methods, all true insider's secrets. Have you ever noticed that insiders in any field have a language of their own? They have a few words that mean much to those on the inside, and which serve to set them apart from others. It is by this language that many people are able to penetrate the inner circle of a special field. Bankers have a language of their own. It's use aids in the precision of their communications with each other, but it also identifies them as part of a group of insiders. Successful real estate people make use of such a language. In the fields of radio, television, newspaper, and magazine advertising there is also a language that insiders use to make their job of communication with others easier—and also to identify those who have served their apprenticeship. There are a few words that shout to insiders that the person using them is on the "inside."

The one phrase we are most concerned with here, and the one which will open the money doors at radio and TV stations and in the advertising offices of big publishers is simply this—P/I. As simple as this may appear, it is truly the "Open Sesame" of the advertising world, and it simply means this—"Per Inquiry." This is abbreviated from its actual meaning which is "per-inquiry advertising."

When you use P/I, you will get your message on the screen, in the press, and on the radio without having to pay the costs that others have had to pay. Obviously, you have the right to scoff. The other popular adage—"You get nothing for nothing" —would seem to apply when we first tell people of this powerful wealth-building technique. And, in a sense you are right. But, let us tell you how a man with an idea used the P/I power to build wealth. This story will serve to introduce you to the secret of P/I profits.

HOW ONE USER GOT $690 WORTH OF FREE ADVERTISING AND MADE $4,120

Walter M. was out of a job and was frantically looking for help to find one. He turned to both employment agencies and executive recruiters. When he looked to the recruiters, he found that they each called themselves something else. An employment agency is an employment agency, but in one state the recruiter was called an executive search house. In another, they might be called management consultants. In other words, there is no consistency in this field.

Walter felt that he might be able to solve his employment problem, help others, and possibly make a lot of money by publishing a directory of these elusive recruiters all over the country. It took a lot of time to research the project, but time was one thing Walter had.

When his directory was assembled, he had it typed in a simple form, and had a local printer produce it for him. It is interesting to note that Walter worked out a deal with this printer whereby the printer supplied the job for a piece of the action. In other words, Walter didn't have to spend a cent to print his directory. All he invested was his time. Sound familiar?

Now, with directory in hand, Walter faced a crisis. He had gotten out the publicity, as we described in Chapter 10. It worked, but once a magazine runs publicity on one product, they will not repeat it. After all, the concept of publicity is news and Walter's directory was no longer news. He had money from sales resulting from the publicity, but not enough to mount the kind of an advertising program that would make him real money.

When we explained the concept of per inquiry advertising to Walter, he was astonished. P/I deals are really "loans" from a publisher, except that no repayment is demanded unless sales are made. Here's what we had Walter do:

- Make a list of every magazine in which he would like to advertise. Obviously, he selected those magazines which executives read because they are the people he had to reach.

- Walter got this list from the Business Publication edition of *Standard Rate and Data* Service. This monthly directory of business, trade, and professional magazines is often available in libraries, but can most readily be found in advertising agencies. Actually, every advertising agency has a subscription. For the promise of future business, you should be able to find an agency willing to let you have a back copy, as Walter did.

- When his list was complete, we had Walter write the following letter describing his *guide,* including a thorough projection of the market, the number of guides he felt could be sold to readers, and the profits to be made.

Advertising Manager
ABC Magazine
City and State

Dear Sir:

We published recently THE GUIDE TO EXECUTIVE RECRUITERS and feel the readers of your publication would form a natural and highly profitable audience for this book. This book includes the names and addresses of 2,500 recruiters, employment counselors, and firms specializing in the search for executive talent. In addition, a 24-page introductory section includes help in preparing a resume that will enhance a person's career experience and make successful interviews more likely. A copy of this GUIDE is enclosed with our compliments so you can form your own judgment of its value to your readers.

On the basis of your circulation among executives, we feel an advertisement in your magazine would sell, on the average, approximately 75 copies a month. At $20 a copy, this would represent an average monthly income of $1,500. We should like to run such an advertisement under the following arrangement that would permit both of us to test the "pulling power" of your magazine:

- We will prepare an advertisement with a keyed coupon for inclusion in an forthcoming issue as space is available;

- The orders will go to you directly, together with all customer remittances;
- You will keep one-half of all money received, and send us the other half with the names and addresses of the persons responding to the advertisement;
- We will ship immediately as your orders are received.

If our assessment of your magazine is correct, and orders do average around 75 copies a month, then each of us will earn $750 a month. According to the latest issue of STANDARD RATE AND DATA, your page rate is $690, so this arrangement can earn you more money than selling advertising space at your regular, published rates.

We feel this arrangement can make substantial profit for both of us working together cooperatively, and we would look forward to a long, continuing relationship.

If there is any additional information we can supply, please do not hesitate to call. We sincerely look forward to working together.

> Very truly yours,
>
> Walter M———
> Publisher

- As the publisher received orders for the $20 directory, he would send the order, along with $10, or half of the amount received for the order, to Walter. Walter would then ship the book and pocket the other $10. In other words, Walter made his money by splitting the price of the book with the publisher. The publisher took the chance of running the ad, feeling that Walter had a good idea; he ran the ad and sold 412 copies. Walter and the magazine split $8,240, or $4,120 each.

- Many publishers will continue to run P/I deals with you as long as they are profitable. If they don't work, of course, the publisher will cut you off.

- Even when a P/I operation is successful, the publisher may sometimes cut you off. Some publishers feel that the P/I deal is a way of proving the "pulling power" of their publication, and that you should go on a pay-as-you-go basis as soon as this fact is proved to you. Or, the decision may be made on the basis of profits the publisher foresees. He may make more money by continuing the P/I program rather than selling the space at his regular rates to you. At this point, you will have to play it by ear. But, in any case, you will now have a product that is trusted and making money. You will be able to afford either deal—and make a lot of money.

HOW YOU CAN BE IN THE COMPANY
OF THE FINANCIAL GIANTS

Even though the situation we just described was built around one man with an idea, the biggest companies in the country use P/I advertising. This is why it is truly the insider's secret of making a fast fortune. When a huge company is willing to negotiate such a deal, you know that it is a powerful method.

The companies that make a lot of use of P/I deals are publishers and others who have a mail order product that can be sold on a one-step basis. By "one-step" we mean a promotion that describes a product and asks for an order at the same time. Most couponed ads you see in magazines are examples of one-steps.

The ad that Walter M. ran for his GUIDE TO EXECUTIVE RECRUITERS was an example of a one-step. When Walter and the publisher of the magazine agreed to a trial P/I deal, Walter made up a full-page ad that started out with a headline that said: "Find the job you want with the help of these 2,500 experts . . . ."

The ad then went into detail about the GUIDE describing all the features so that a reader of the magazine got a very clear picture of what he was buying. As a final selling point, Walter included an iron-clad money-back guarantee—if the reader of the GUIDE was dissatisfied with the book for any reason, he could return it within thirty days and get an immediate refund of his purchase price. Finally, a coupon made it easy to order the GUIDE by mail. It was just such an ad that pulled in orders for 412 copies of the GUIDE and put Walter in the mail order publishing business.

Some ads you see, generally small classified ads, are known as "two-steps." They are so called because it takes two separate steps to sell to the customer. In a small ad it is impossible to name the features of your product, to spell out guarantees fully, or even to describe adequately the product. In such a case, a small "teaser" ad can be run such as:

> *MAKE BIG MONEY from your home in the export-import business. Low investment; no handling of merchandise. Free details. Write Box____, Address, State, Zip.*

Since there is no obligation on the part of the reader to get "free details" the response to such ads is generally high. When the advertiser gets the inquiries, he then has to perform step two in the selling effort; he sends the person a direct mail piece that describes the product fully, together with a coupon or order card. Naturally, only a certain percentage of the inquiries will be converted into orders, so the expense of the original ad, the cost of the direct mail follow-ups, and the conversion rate all have to be figured before deciding whether the campaign was profitable.

It is impossible to get a P/I deal which will be attractive to a magazine publisher on a "two step" basis. The complications of keeping track of inquiries and conversions into orders just isn't worth the effort. However, if you have some experience with your product and its acceptance in the marketplace, you can make some estimate of your conversion rate and offer a publisher a set price for each inquiry forwarded to you. In other words, the original teaser ad carries an address that gets the inquiry back to the cooperating publisher. He sends you the inquiries together with a bill based on so much per inquiry. In fact, this was the original intent of P/I advertising and is the reason it is called "per-inquiry" advertising.

Walter M. made several such deals with other publishers who were willing to give him small space on a straight per-inquiry basis. Here's how one such deal worked out for Walter:

Walter offered publishers a flat $1 per inquiry received. One publisher ran three small ads which resulted in 350 inquiries which were forwarded to Walter.

Cost of inquiries (350 @ $1 each) $350
Cost of follow-up mailings (350 @ 20¢ each) 70
Total sales cost $420

Of the 350 inquiries received, Walter was able to convert
10 percent, or 35, into cash orders. This is not an unusual conversion rate when using the two-step process to sell a product
by mail. Therefore, Walter's balance sheet looked like this:

Total income (35 orders @ $20 each) $700
Less sales cost of ads and follow-ups 420
Balance $280

Out of this balance, Walter still had to pay for the printing
of his GUIDE. These ran him $3 apiece, including the cost of
a carton to mail the GUIDE to the customer and book-rate
postage. So:

Balance $280
Cost of product (35 @ $3 each) 105
Left over for profit $175

Now, $175 is not a fantastic profit by itself. But, Walter was
able to expand these P/I deals over the course of a year or two
with many other magazines. Ultimately, he was averaging
about 3,000 inquiries a month and grossing $6,000 a month.
Even though he was paying $3,000 a month for these inquiries,
he still showed a neat monthly profit of $1,500. Best of all,
handling the inquiries and orders was eventually done by several part-time workers he hired in the neighborhood. Even
though they cost him $300, he still had $1,200 clean profit for
himself each month—truly an automatic income!

Later, he was introduced to a list broker who showed great
interest in the inquiry list Walter was building up month by
month. In return for a broker's commission, the list broker
took the inquiries after Walter used them for his conversion
efforts. The inquiries were put on a computerized list and
rented to other noncompeting mail order operators.

A $25,000-A-YEAR AUTOMATIC INCOME IS POSSIBLE

Inquiry lists such as Walter's usually rent for about $25 per
1,000 names. Walter had about 35,000 names available for
rental and his broker did a good job promoting them. Soon, he

was averaging about two rentals of the complete list each month. This earned $1,750 a month just in rental fees alone. The broker took 40 percent of these proceeds for maintaining the list on a computer and for actively promoting the list to other mail order users. This left Walter with 60 percent or $1,050 for doing nothing but letting his list out for rental.

This $1,050, when added to the $1,200 a month profit he was making on the sale of his GUIDE totaled out to $2,250 a month *profit.* That's $27,000 a year—*automatically*! Needless to say, Walter never did get around to looking for a job working for somebody else.

HOW YOU CAN GET YOUR PRODUCT SOLD ON TV WITHOUT SPENDING A CENT ON TIME

Most TV advertising is for nationally made and distributed products such as automobiles and food. The commercials are aimed at getting you into the store to buy the advertised product. But, on local television—those stations not affiliated with one of the big networks—you will also see many ads for products that appear to be sold through the television station. Usually the ads are for records, books, or specialty products; but in all cases, the announcer implores the viewers to send their money directly for the product. And, invariably, the address is that of the TV station, with a keyed box number. The keyed box number identifies the station running the ad and the time-slot, and the order is picked up by the station.

The TV station is not in the mail order business, but it is simply applying the P/I principle to its merchandising. It works the same way as the P/I deals we have just described as being used by magazines and newspaper publishers. And, for impulse items, it is one of the most effective ways to sell merchandise.

HOW YOU CAN GET YOUR PRODUCT ON TELEVISION

Don't be discouraged by the competition you seem to have in advertisers on TV. The big companies spend millions of dollars annually on television advertising to get people into the stores. The auto companies, the food companies, clothing manufacturers, cosmetics people, and many others take up most of the time on TV all with the one goal of getting the viewer into the store where he will buy the product advertised.

But, if you will follow TV ads closely, you will discover something rather interesting. The channels affiliated with NBC, CBS, and ABC, the network channels, have the bulk of national advertising, in addition to the well-known network shows. The local channels usually run a lot of movies, re-runs of popular past shows, cartoon shows for kids, *plus* a lot of local advertising. The local advertising can be for furniture stores, discount houses, automobile dealers, and similar retailers. These local channels also run a lot of mail order advertising; this is how to discover the channels most likely to accept P/I advertising. Don't waste your time on channels affiliated with the big networks; you'd be lucky to even get a reply to your letter.

Walter M. took a stab at P/I advertising with his GUIDE TO EXECUTIVE RECRUITERS on the airways. STANDARD RATE AND DATA Service publishes guides to radio and TV stations. Through a friend at an advertising agency, Walter got a copy and started to do some homework. He wrote to the U.S. Department of Labor and got the latest statistics on unemployment in various cities around the country. He matched the cities with the highest unemployment rates with stations listed in his SRDS that were *not* network stations. His reasoning was simple: a P/I spot on an early morning news program would reach a lot of persons getting up and setting out job hunting. The early news announcer could read the commercial during a break in the program, and a simple slide, flashed on the screen could show the viewer where to send his order.

All these thoughts were outlined in Walter's letters to the stations, and eventually he had a half dozen stations running TV ads for his GUIDE on a 50-50 P/I deal. His outlay for promotion was virtually nil; yet his efforts sold 800 books. This was $16,000 worth of business split between Walter and the TV stations.

By watching the shows regularly during the years, you can get the feel of when these ads are run, and consequently when time is available that you might use profitably. Late in the evening, early mornings, and after holidays are about the most inactive periods for paid TV advertising. Knowing this, you can approach a local TV station and ask for a P/I deal. The chances are very good that you will be able to swing a money-making P/I deal if you hit the station with a sound product to sell directly from a commercial.

You will further your cause if you have done your homework carefully and can tell the station manager that you know he has lean times late in the evening and early in the morning. If you can show him how a free commercial can make money for the station (as well as you) he will snap up the idea. It is done every day, and there is no reason why you shouldn't climb on the bandwagon. This is just one more example of how you can use the concept of "Total Borrowing' to build wealth quickly.

HOW YOU CAN HAVE A COMMERCIAL PREPARED FREE

The cost to prepare some of the automobile commercials often runs into millions of dollars. A simple cosmetic commercial can cost hundreds of thousands. Don't let these numbers frighten you. But, don't expect the station to create a commercial of this magnitude for you either.

Most P/I commercials prepared for airing on local TV are written by the station promotion staff and are delivered by a station announcer. The announcer will have your product to display while he is delivering the commercial, and he will emphasize the cost and the address to use when ordering your product. In fact, he will emphasize the address to the point where you might become annoyed at his repetition. But, this is done with a reason. People seldom have pencil and paper near the TV set, and will often miss the first mention of the address. By repeating the address, the announcer insures that people who are interested in ordering will be able to get a paper and pencil in time to make a note of the important details.

Actually, this kind of local advertising can be very effective, even when it is sandwiched in between two other commercials, each costing thousands of dollars. The reason for this is quite simple. The P/I commercial is usually delivered by a local announcer, or the host of a local show. Over the years, this man has developed a following of people who believe in him. When he delivers your commercial, his regular viewers will often respond to the tune of many orders.

We mentioned previously that Walter M. sold 800 copies of his GUIDE with P/I deals on TV. Of that 800, about 300 were sold on one show over a period of time. This was an early morning newscast whose announcer had developed a loyal following by concentrating on the weather, time, and notes of local interest. Grim world happenings he left for the announcer coming on at 8 a.m. As a result, he had high interest and believability when he urged readers who were job hunting to send for the GUIDE.

HOW YOU CAN GET YOUR PRODUCT SOLD
OVER THE RADIO

Actually, it is often easier to get P/I deals with local radio stations than it is with TV stations. Most TV stations are part of vast networks, with the result that the local stations may have very little control over its programming. All of the programs and commercials come from the headquarters station, and there is often little time available for local spot commercials. You will be able to get them, but you will find the competition a bit heavier than you will find with locally owned and controlled radio stations.

There are many local radio stations that are totally independent, and will respond very warmly to the suggestion of P/I advertising deals. The network affiliates will also run P/I deals, but it is often more difficult to get to them.

Your approach can be a little different than that we suggested for TV. Your approach to the TV station, as we described, should be made on the basis of using time slots not filled during the lean times of early morning and late evening. However, on radio, you would be better advised to approach the station on the basis of the best time to reach the specific audience you know will want to buy your products.

For example, if you are trying to sell a product specifically to women, you would want to get on the air during the daylight hours when many women are at home and listening to programs directed specifically to them. Try to reach the male audience in the evening when the news broadcasts are on, during the weekend when local sports events are being broadcast, or in the morning when men are listening to radios driving to work.

Walter tried this tack in a modestly successful effort to get P/I deals on radio. This is the letter he wrote to stations he got out of SRDS:

> Advertising Manager
> Station WXXX
> City and State
>
> Dear Sir:
>
> We recently published THE GUIDE TO EXECUTIVE RE-CRUITERS and feel certain portions of your total listening audience would form a natural and highly profitable audience for this book. This book includes the names and addresses of 2,500 recruiters, employment counselors, and firms specializing in the search for executive talent. In addition, a 24-page introductory section includes help in preparing a resume that will enhance a person's career experience, and make successful interviews more likely. A copy of this GUIDE is enclosed with our compliments so you can form your own judgment of its value to your listeners.
>
> On the basis of your listening audience, particularly among men driving to work during the hours between 6:30 a.m. and 8:30 a.m., we feel a one-minute commercial would sell, on the average, five copies per announcement. At $20 a copy, this would represent an income of $100 per commercial. Ten commercials a week within these time limits could earn $1,000. We should like to run such a commercial under the following arrangement that would permit both of us to test the "pulling power" of such commercials on your station:
>
> - We will prepare a one-minute script for broadcast by your announcer;
> - All orders will go to you directly, together with customer remittances;
> - You will keep one-half of all money received, and send us the other half with the names and addresses of the persons responding to the offer;
> - We will ship immediately as your orders are received.

If our assessment of your listeners is correct, and orders do average around fifty copies a week, then each of us will earn $500 a month. According to the latest issue of STANDARD RATE AND DATA, your rate at the time suggested runs $35 a minute. This arrangement can earn you $500 for the same time that would normally be sold for only $350.

We feel this arrangement can make a substantial profit for both of us working together cooperatively, and we would look forward to a long, continuing relationship.

If there is any additional information we can supply, please do not hesitate to call. We sincerely look forward to working together.

> Very truly yours,
>
> Walter M-------
> Publisher

USING THE MAGIC OF P/I ADVERTISING

As you can see, P/I advertising is truly the insider's secret of making money with TV, radio, and magazines. It works, it will continue to work, and you can take advantage of it. But, always prepare carefully before you approach anyone with an idea. The people who run the stations and magazines have been the route. They know what offers work and what offers will not work. If you prepare your case carefully, and can show the people who make the decisions that you have a good product and that you know when, where, and how to promote it with their station or magazine, you can literally get millions of dollars worth of "free" advertising. To help you prepare your case here are a few things to consider when you think that you have a hot proposition:

- *Price.* As with any mail order product, the price should be competitive with the price for a similar product if it is already being sold in a store. If possible, it should be a little lower than competition. And, because you are asking people to send you money without actually being able to see, feel, hear, or touch the merchandise, the price will have to be relatively low. Watch your TV set and see just what prices are going in your area for direct sale merchandise. You will have to price to make a profit, of course. Because every situation is different, it will be impossible for us to give you any hard and fast rules. But, remember to include all costs when you price your product. Little things like miscalculating the cost of postage to mail your product out can make the difference between profit and loss. There is often more than a 50 percent mark-up in products sold through the mail. This may seem like a lot, but selling costs are high and many mail order companies thrive on as little as 5 percent net profit, derived from this 50 percent mark-up.

Go back to the cost analysis Walter M. made on his product starting on page ____ . Notice how he figured in cost of inquiries, cost of follow-ups, postage, cartonning, and the like. A common failing among beginners is to neglect any figure for overhead. In the beginning, your overhead will be trifling; but you should have enough left over in your profit figure to eventually be able to afford a certain overhead. After all, like Walter, you will soon want to hire others to do the drudge work like answering inquiries and filling orders. You will recall that this cost Walter an additional $300 a month.

- *Guarantee.* A money-back guarantee is important. Most mail order products are sold this way, and to be successful in P/I advertising, you must consider a strong money-back guarantee. Again, you are asking people to send you money for products that they have only seen on a TV screen, or heard described on the radio. The clincher in your sales message must be a guarantee to promptly refund the customer's money. Actually, this is not as fearful as it sounds. Walter offered an iron-clad, no-questions-asked, 30-day money-back guarantee on all his offers. His overall reject rate —those people who returned the GUIDE and asked for refunds—averaged out to 7 percent of total sales. This is fairly typical of the reject rate you will get, unless your advertising is so misleading that your customers are disappointed when the merchandise arrives. This is the best advice available: be enthusiastic, but honest, in describing your product; give a strong guarantee; and you will be surprised at how this can increase your sales without causing you to lose money on returned merchandise.

- *General appeal.* Your product must have a general appeal if it is to be accepted for P/I advertising on radio or television. Both are mass media, trying to please everybody. And, so should your product. It should have a wide appeal, and be the kind of impulse product people buy at first encounter, rather than the kind of product that requires further thinking. If you have a product that appeals to a limited audience, you should try for P/I deals with the magazines that cover your market or at times when you will find a likely radio or TV audience. For example, it would be difficult to get fishing tackle advertised on local radio or TV, but it would be a snap to work out a P/I deal with either a local or national sporting magazine.

- *Make it easy to ship.* Books, records, and the like are easy to ship through the mail. In fact, books go by a special rate that is considerably lower than all other postal rates. It would be hard to ship a fishing rod through the mail unless it were collapsable. It is very difficult to ship perishable food unless you go to the expense of special dry-ice containers. Our point is purposely obvious; before you get too far with your P/I arrangements, make sure that you will be able to put your products in the mail easily and inexpensively. And, if you are depending on a supplier to have products sent to you on time, start "hounding" him long before the scheduled shipping date. When people send money through the mail, they can get pretty upset if it takes more than a few weeks to get what they ordered.

- *Have another product ready in the wings.* Your first

sale of the P/I advertised product should only be a stepping stone to many more sales.

- *Be sure to compile a list of buyers . . . and what they bought.* You can use this list to sell other products you will add to your line at a later date. Try to add products which have the same appeal as the products already sold. There is no one who is easier to sell to than a person who has already bought something from you. If you can possibly have other products to sell, be sure to include printed sheets on these products with the merchandise you ship as a result of your P/I advertising. When you get orders on these other products, your sales cost will be almost zero—which means that you will have most of the profits to keep for yourself.

Now you can really begin to see why this "insiders" secret has been kept under wraps. Only those few who know of it have used it and they continue to use it to make money for themselves and for the stations and publications. But, now that we have exposed it to you, you can make use of the power of time and space to build your own personal fortune.

CHECKLIST OF TECHNIQUES TO USE TIME AND SPACE TO BUILD A FORTUNE

1. You can get P/I deals from newspapers, magazines, radio and television stations.
2. You can use P/I advertising whether you are a small basement operation, or a multimillion dollar company. It's the ideas that count here.
3. Time and space will not cost you a cent. You pay only when—and if—you make money. The gamble is completely eliminated. Others have to buy the time and space, regardless of whether or not they make money with their program.
4. TV and radio stations will prepare your commercial without charge.
5. Make sure your product is easy to ship, is priced to sell and turn you a profit, has a strong guarantee, has

general appeal for radio and TV, and has specific appeal for special interest magazines.

6. Always have another product ready to sell to the people who are already buying from you.

13

GET MONEY — AND MORE —
FROM THE GOVERNMENT

The day you decide to go into business you acquire a very important partner who will be part of your enterprise forever. There is absolutely no way you can avoid this partnership. You can't fire him and neither can you ever buy him out and be independent. Because you will have to live with him forever, it makes sense that you learn how to work together. Better yet, you should do everything possible to make this silent partner an active member of your team . . . someone who will work with you every step of the way helping you to succeed.

Who is this partner? You've probably guessed his name—Uncle Sam. He will be a demanding partner, ever alert to get his share at tax time. But, he can also be the most valuable partner a person can have in business. His resources are unlimited, and he stands ready to give you outright, or let you borrow, just about everything you need in order to make a success of your enterprise.

In this chapter we will tell you some of the ways Uncle Sam can help you become more successful in your business. We will tell you of the many agencies of the Government set up specifically to help a small businessman such as yourself. And, if you should think that all these programs are designed for the big corporations, you will change your mind when you read about ordinary people who prospered when they asked for Uncle Sam's help.

THE GOVERNMENT WANTS TO HELP YOU MAKE MORE MONEY

When you pay your taxes, you may have the feeling that all Uncle Sam is interested in is taking a share of your hard-earned money. If you feel that way, it's because you haven't learned how to make him work for the money. Once you learn how to get the most out of your silent partner, the money you pay will be well spent in your estimation—the same as if you paid a nominal salary to a valuable, loyal, and productive employee.

Curiously enough, the Government is actually very much interested in your making a lot of money. It's to their advantage—the more money you make, the more they stand to collect. Official Government policy is to encourage business to prosper, especially small businesses, and an incredible number and variety of Government programs have been developed for just this purpose. Any businessman who closes his eyes to the many benefits available to him is simply closing off a doorway to opportunity.

Charlie C. almost missed his big chance in life because he was unaware of the many kinds of help available to the small businessman. Charlie was handy with tools and made a fair living for a number of years as a cabinetmaker. He ran a small shop that dealt with custom-made cabinets and built-in furniture. His dream was to own a factory someday where he could manufacture furniture kits and sell them nationally through mail order ads in various home and garden magazines. But— this took money. Big money. So for years, Charlie kept saving, hoping to accumulate enough capital to start on his dream.

Actually, Charlie could never have saved enough money to start his manufacturing operation because production machines are so expensive. Fortunately, Charlie heard about an SBIC through a friend who worked in a bank. An SBIC is an abbreviation for Small Business Investment Corporation.

Basically, an SBIC is a privately owned and privately operated small business investment company that has been licensed by the Small Business Administration (an arm of the U.S. Government) to provide equity capital and long-term loans to small firms. In addition to money, an SBIC can often furnish management advice to inexperienced businessmen. Because Charlie knew woodworking, was ambitious, and had a record of hard work and limited success in his small business, he was able to interest an SBIC in providing him with a small business loan amounting to $150,000. Charlie could never have saved this kind of money, and with it he did the following:

- Signed a lease on a vacant building that was easily converted into a place suitable for woodworking operations.
- Bought the production equipment he needed at favorable rates because he had the money to make substantial down-payments.
- Ordered his raw materials in economic, large-lot sizes.
- Was able to engage the services of advertising and marketing experts with particular expertise in mail order selling.

The result: it wasn't long before Charlie was handling the kind of money he never dared to dream about. And, it wasn't long either before that original $150,000 was repaid and Charlie saw his business hit the magic one-million dollar gross sales figure.

In Charlie's case, Uncle Sam was a very important partner and essential to his success. True, an SBIC is a private corporation, but the Federal Government encourages these small business investment companies to help small businessmen with growing pains. It does so by guaranteeing the loans. With little risk, even a private company will be glad to put its money in enterprises that normally might look a bit risky. Generally, this is typical of the way Uncle Sam will help you, a small businessman, with your many money problems. Rather than an outright grant, gift, or free loan from the Government, you'll find the help you need at a variety of private and semi-official agencies that have the backing of the Government to help persons such as yourself. This is an important thing to bear in mind; you won't get anything for nothing or just for the asking. But you will get a lot of help if you show you are capable of using it. Charlie did, and his loan was quick to come.

THOUSANDS OF SPECIALISTS ARE WAITING TO HELP YOU

Each year, the Government spends millions upon millions of dollars doing research of one sort or another. Much of this research is in the area of small business, and the results are published in countless volumes, reports, and other publications. With the exception of classified documents relating to our national defense, all of this information is available to you at little or no cost.

For example, here are some typical titles of Government reports that you can use as a shortcut to success:

Small Business Location and Layout

Effective Advertising

Marketing Research

Managing for Profits

Handbook of Small Business Finance

Starting and Managing a Building Business . . . a Retail Store . . . a Car-wash . . . or any of dozens of other types of businesses.

Selling by Mail Order

Financing . . . Short and Long Term Needs

Doing Business with the Federal Government

Collecting Past Due Accounts Without Losing Customers

Handicrafts and Home Businesses

. . . and literally hundreds upon hundreds more

How and where do you start? That's easy. The first thing to do is to write to the Superintendent of Documents, U.S. Government Printing Office, Washington, D.C. 20402, and request a copy of *A Survey of Federal Government Publications of Interest to Small Businessmen.* The price of this publication is only forty-five cents, and it lists many of the books, booklets, pamphlets, leaflets, and reports published by various Government agencies which are most likely to be of value to the small businessman. Some of the publications are for sale at very nominal prices, while many others are available free.

HOW YOU CAN GET HELP FROM GOVERNMENT AGENCIES

The various Government agencies can provide you with help on specific problems relating to their area of interest. Here is a quick overview of some important ways they can help you:

DEPARTMENT OF AGRICULTURE, WASHINGTON, D.C. 20250

This agency helps both farmers and consumers. It can help you get started in many types of food businesses such as co-operatives, food lockers, food handling, forest products for profit, and so on.

DEPARTMENT OF COMMERCE, WASHINGTON, D.C. 20230

This agency includes, among others, the Bureaus of Census and is the nation's "answer man" when it comes to facts, figures, trends, etc. It publishes all sorts of directories and other statistical information important to marketers. Here you can find out the location of manufacturing plants throughout the country classified by size and location, guides to exporting, franchise data, sources of credit information, and more.

DEPARTMENT OF DEFENSE, WASHINGTON, D.C. 20301

If you have anything to do with supplying items for the military, this is the agency to contact. In particular, ask for the publications on *Selling to the Military, How to Do Business with the Defense Supply Agency,* and *Product Qualification and Qualified Products Lists.* Remember—the Government is committed to a policy of buying a certain percentage of products from small businesses, and there is no reason why you can't go after your share.

FEDERAL TRADE COMMISSION, WASHINGTON, D.C. 20580

Most of the material available from this arm of the Government is quite technical, and is designed for those with legal training. However, they do issue a publication you can read with profit. It is entitled: "Guides Against Deceptive Advertising, Labeling, and Pricing." While we wouldn't suggest you try to be your own lawyer, this one publication will go a long way toward keeping you out of trouble. It will certainly make your lawyer's job a lot easier (and his fee a lot lower) if you observe the basic rules and regulations that are readily understood by the layman.

Dick R. ran a small mail order publishing business. He published one small book that dealt with an important construction code. The importance of knowing the Government regulations on fair pricing was brought home to him when a large catalogue house showed interest in his publication and wanted to include it in their promotion of "how-to" books.

Dick was ready to throw his discount schedule out the window in order to land this big account. Then he remembered the rule of the Federal Trade Commission that says you can't show favoritism in your dealings with similar customers. He swallowed hard and told the buyer that in all fairness he had to abide by his standard discount. Not only did Dick stay on the right side of the law, he earned the respect of this important customer and landed the order by this fact alone!

GOVERNMENT PRINTING OFFICE, WASHINGTON, D.C. 20402

We mentioned previously *A Survey of Federal Government Publications of Interest to the Small Businessman*; however, this is only one of scores of publications available from this office that can help you. Write to them with any question you have and it is quite likely they will send back lists of publications available that can supply just the help you need. One hint to get best service here: be as specific as you can in your request. If you asked for "items of interest to a small businessman," chances are you would be disappointed in their selections because they simply wouldn't know where to begin.

You will, however, get a lot of help if you ask such questions as:

- What do I need to know to open a retail store?
- How do I establish prices in a service business such as a car-wash?

- How do I go about developing and marketing a new product?

DEPARTMENT OF HEALTH, EDUCATION AND WELFARE, WASHINGTON, D.C. 20201

The Social Security Administration is part of this agency and is located in Baltimore, Md. 21235. If you are self-employed in a business of your own, you can still protect yourself with Social Security benfits. Or, if you grow to the point where you have people working for you, you will have to observe regulations in this area. The agency in Washington can give you help on many aspects of health services for employees, pollution laws, running nursing homes and day care centers, and more.

DEPARTMENT OF HOUSING AND URBAN DEVELOPMENT (HUD), WASHINGTON, D.C. 20310

The Federal Housing Administration is part of this agency, which can give you a lot of information relating to government programs in this area. If you want to improve property in blighted neighborhoods, open a nursing home, or engage in any type of activity relating to housing, get in touch with them at an early stage of your planning.

DEPARTMENT OF THE INTERIOR, WASHINGTON, D.C. 20240

The Bureau of Outdoor Recreation is part of this agency and is probably very little known by opportunity seekers. Yet, through this agency, you can get help in developing lakes, camp grounds, ski resorts, and just about any other type of outdoor facility that can be used by the public. If you're a fishing enthusiast and want to seek your fortune from the water, you should contact the Bureau of Commercial Fisheries.

DEPARTMENT OF LABOR, WASHINGTON, D.C. 20210

Once you hire your first employee, you're involved with *labor,* and you had better start off right. This agency publishes an enormous amount of material, much of it in the form of studies and directories that are useful to forecasters in industry. For the small businessman, they provide valuable help by explaining various labor laws and acts that you will have to observe. These cover wages and hours, working conditions, safety, and the rest. If you want government help in training workers, this agency can help you.

LIBRARY OF CONGRESS, COPYRIGHT OFFICE, WASHINGTON, D.C. 20540

This book that you are now reading is protected by copyright. No one can copy or reprint it without permission of the copyright owner—a fundamental protection guaranteed by the Federal Government. If you produce any printed material in the course of your business—booklets, forms, illustrations, or whatever—you can enjoy the same copyright protection enjoyed by the nation's largest publishers. The forms are simple to fill out and the fees to file your applications are quite modest. However, you must file the correct form for the particular work you want to protect; different forms are used for books, articles, films, speeches, and the like. Write to The Registrar of the Copyright Office and he'll give you all the information you need, together with the appropriate forms.

NATIONAL SCIENCE FOUNDATION, WASHINGTON, D.C. 20550

The National Science Foundation can give you help if you want to know what Federal funds are available for research, development, and other scientific activities.

DEPARTMENT OF THE NAVY, WASHINGTON, D.C. 20360

If you have anything that you think you can sell to the Navy, ask for a copy of *Selling to Navy Contractors.*

DEPARTMENT OF THE TREASURY, INTERNAL REVENUE SERVICE, WASHINGTON, D.C. 20224

This is the "ouch" department once a year when you fill out your tax return. But remember one thing—regardless how trifling it may be, you have the legal right to take every penny of deductions allowed by law. The trouble is that most people don't fully know what they're entitled to, and overpay their taxes. Even if you have a professional fill out your tax returns, he can only work with the information you have collected during the year and have made available to him. The first thing you should do when you start a business is to get a copy of *Tax Guide for Small Business*. It will save you money on your taxes.

SMALL BUSINESS ADMINISTRATION, WASHINGTON, D.C. 20416

It is truly impossible to estimate how many small businessmen owe their financial success to help they got in one form or another from the Small Business Administration. There are local offices of this agency located in major cities and towns all over the country. At these offices, you can talk to someone and get advice, pick up scores of publications on every aspect of small business, and get reliable information on the major Government programs designed specifically for the small businessman. Here are some of the programs they administer:

Business Loans. If a businessman needs money and cannot borrow it locally at reasonable rates, the Small Business Administration can often help. While SBA does not make direct loans, it will work with a local bank and guarantee the loan. In effect, Uncle Sam becomes your "co-signer."

Pool Loans. The SBA will loan money to groups of businessmen who wish to cooperate in the purchase of raw materials, equipment, or establish some sort of cooperative facility.

Economic Opportunity Loans. This program provides management help and financial assistance to disadvantaged persons.

Development Company Loans. The SBA helps small businessmen acquire land, and helps to pay for the construction, conversion, and expansion of existing buildings.

Disaster Loans. The SBA will make emergency loans at low-interest rates to victims of natural disasters. These loans can be used to repair or replace damaged structures, furnishings, machinery, and inventory. They also offer loans to businesses that are displaced by Federal projects such as roads.

Procurement Assistance. Relatively little is known of the help SBA can give businesses in getting their names on Government lists of "preferred bidders." Government purchases, by law, must be made from small businessmen for certain portions of contracts. You have every right to go after these Government contracts, and the SBA can help you here.

Among the Government Agencies, the Small Business Administration is probably the most prolific as a publisher. The books and booklets they distribute free, or at a very low cost, range from *ABC's of Borrowing* to *Woodworking Shops*. The free publications cover:

- *Management Aids For Small Manufacturers* — discussions of the various phases of managing a small manufacturing business including accounting, financial management, personnel management, and purchasing and market research.

- *Technical Aids for Small Manufacturers* — facts on significant developments in materials, processes, equipment, and maintenance.

- *Small Business Bibliographies* — reference sources for business owners and managers, and those just starting out in business.

- *Small Marketers Aids* — discussions of various phases of managing a small retail service or wholesale business, including advertising, competitive strategy, controlling, and selling.

In addition, for a small fee, you can purchase SBA booklets on general good practices in starting and managing various small businesses. In the small space available in this chapter, it is impossible to even begin to mention the various titles. If you have questions or problems, don't hesitate to get in touch with your local office for a personal consultation, or write to the addresses we've given you.

BUILDING A VACATION PARADISE AND A BOOMING BUSINESS WITH GOVERNMENT HELP

Your Government recognizes the importance of recreation in American life and is prepared to help you and everyone else to enjoy all the natural beauty and recreational potential of our public lands. Do you enjoy skiing? The Government runs ski areas in various National Parks. But—did you know that this same Government will also lease public lands to a private individual, such as yourself, to *build* a ski run? Not only will it lease the land, but various agencies will help you get a loan to develop the area, build the lifts, and construct all the service buildings and lodges needed to attract paying customers.

Or, look at the case of a farmer who had a 40-acre field at one end of his farm that never paid out when planted with cash crops. With Government help and advice, he turned this field into a shooting preserve. During hunting season, hunters come in droves and pay handsomely for the privilege of flushing out the birds.

Several departments and agencies are involved in outdoor recreation projects. As a start you should contact the Department of Agriculture previously mentioned. This agency can give you:

- *Technical help.* Government experts will help you design the best type of recreational facility for the land you have in mind, whether you own it or plan to lease it from the Government. These same experts will make on-the-spot surveys and tell you what to plant, how to prevent erosion, and how to take full advantage of the natural resources.

- *Financial help.* You can get loans for recreational projects, whether you're applying as an individual or part of a community group.

- *Management help.* Again, Government help is available to you to help prevent mistakes in running your recreational enterprise.

So far, we have talked almost exclusively about Federal help available to you if you want to make money in the booming recreation business. Many of the states and individual counties have programs to help you, too. The county agent is an important person in farm country. But he also performs an important service to suburbanites living near cities, far away from a farm. If you are planning a golf driving range, for example, he can tell you what kind of grass to plant, what to do for windbreaks, and how to prevent your investment from turning into a muddy swamp when it rains. Our advice is simple: get out your telephone directory and look up all the local, county, and state offices that are listed. Even a simple run-down like this will give you hints on where to ask additional questions.

USING THE NEAR-FORGOTTEN HOMESTEAD ACT TO GET FREE LAND

Over a hundred years ago, Congress passed, and President Lincoln signed, a law designed to encourage settlement of our Western frontiers. It was called the Homestead Act and is taught to every schoolchild in his history class. What most people don't realize is that the Homestead Act is still very much in force. Basically, any American citizen can settle on 160 acres of available public land, farm all or only a part of it, and become the owner after five years. The only cost is a small filing fee for the legal documents.

During the century the law has been in effect most of the desirable lands in the West have been taken. However, now that Alaska is a state, there are new opportunities for home-steading there. Farming in Alaska can be a much different business than farming in our warmer states. But, farm products are priced high in Alaska because they have to be shipped long distances. Surely this suggests an opportunity for an energetic person.

HOW TO ACQUIRE PUBLIC LANDS AT LOW COST

If you would like to acquire a smaller piece of property, the Government holds regular sales on these. Again, most of this property is way out from civilization, which makes it all the more intriguing as a vacation hideaway, hunting club, camp-site, or even a place for a store if there is enough recreational traffic to warrant it. Often, this land is sold for a few dollars an acre. If you want to know what is available, write to the Bureau of Land Management in Washington, D.C. For sixty cents a year, you can subscribe to *Our Public Lands,* which describes the availability of tracts for sale. Send your order to the Superintendent of Documents, Washington, D.C. 20402.

MAKING A PROFIT ON GOVERNMENT SURPLUS PROPERTY

The Government regularly disposes of its surplus property, and you can bid on the items just as well as the next fellow.

Some people buy surplus as an inexpensive way of getting adaptable machinery, tools, or equipment. Certain types of government vehicles can be adapted for recreational use, particularly important if you decide to develop a recreational area for profit. Other opportunity seekers simply buy Government surplus at low, "wholesale" bids, and then re-sell the merchandise at retail either through store outlets or by mail order.

Here is the story of Neil S. who bid ten cents each for 100 "flight calculators" thinking they were little cardboard dial-type affairs. Neil was happy to learn that for a total of $10 he was the successful bidder, but almost fainted when he discovered the "flight calculators" turned out to be very sophisticated electronic devices! He later sold them for $200 apiece making a profit of just about $20,000. This story is true, but you shouldn't dream of becoming rich by such a lucky accident. Rather, if you know what you're looking for, know what to spend, and most important—know what you can sell your purchase for—then you can prosper in Government surplus. Your first step is to know what is being declared surplus and put up for sale. Contact the Defense Surplus Bidders Control Office, The Federal Center, Battle Creek, Michigan 49016.

HOW TO GET ON PREFERRED BIDDER'S LISTS
FOR GOVERNMENT PURCHASES

As a small businessman, you have certain privileges in selling products or services to the Federal Government. A certain portion of Government contracts have to be let to bidders coming from the ranks of small businessmen. But, you have to know what the government is buying, what it has paid in the past for similar items, and when it plans on buying again. All this information is readily available; the place to start is your local office of the Small Business Administration.

The SBA not only helps you get on bidders' lists, but helps you in other ways. For example:

- SBA is a clearinghouse of information on getting on bidders' lists of the various government agencies. They will tell you which agencies are most likely to need the services or product you sell and how to go about getting on the bidders' list for that agency.

- SBA maintains a file of small firms and their capabilities. If a government agency has some need, SBA can quickly refer that agency to a small businessman who can supply the item or service.
- SBA can issue a "certificate of competency" to you, so that buying agencies of the Government know you have the capability to fulfill a particular contract.

If you want to know if you can sell to the Government, simply ask the SBA office to show you the latest copy of the *U.S. Government Purchasing, Specifications, and Sales Directory.* This directory lists the products and services bought by the Federal Government, tells which agencies buy particular products, and lists the purchasing offices that should be contacted by persons interested in selling specific items to the Government. Once you've decided you can sell to the Government, ask the agency for the necessary forms to fill out and file. This will put you on the bidders' list and whenever that particular agency has need for the items you supply, you'll receive an invitation to bid. If you sell some patented or otherwise exclusive item, you're almost assured of getting the order every time. In such cases, bidding is eliminated and a price is negotiated with the single supplier.

STARTING AN INTERNATIONAL BUSINESS WITH GOVERNMENT HELP

The Department of Commerce mentioned previously can be of enormous help to the small businessman who wants to get his product into overseas sales channels. The Office of International Regional Economics provides businessmen with all kinds of information on marketing in over a hundred different countries, and helps exporters find new outlets abroad. The Bureau of International Business Operations can get your products displayed at overseas trade fairs. Both of these agencies can be reached at the U.S. Department of Commerce, Washington, D.C. 20230.

Everyone complains about their taxes, and how the Government seems to be growing bigger and bigger each day. Let's face facts: unless you want to make a career in politics, there is probably little you personally can do to reverse this trend. Meanwhile, you certainly should take advantage of all the benefits being provided with your tax dollars. Don't make the mistake of thinking that all that Government money being spent is for "the other guy." You can be on the receiving end if you will simply take the time to investigate all the opportunities the Government makes available to you. Here's some help:

CHECKLIST OF MAJOR GOVERNMENT BUSINESS HELPS

- The Government wants *you* to make money in your business enterprise; therefore, don't be shy about going to the Government for help.

- There are thousands of specialists in dozens of Government agencies ready to help you with your questions or problems; use them.

- Get to know your Government; write to the various agencies and departments we mentioned in this chapter.

- The Small Business Administration is the logical starting point for most of your problems; get to know them either by visiting the local office or by writing to Washington.

- An outright grant or loan from the Government is unlikely; but you will find the Government helpful in getting a loan through private sources.

- Don't waste time trying to "re-discover the wheel" in your business; the SBA and other Government agencies have spent millions of dollars to accumulate and publish information. It is virtually certain that any problem you face is covered in some report they have handy.

14

TECHNIQUES YOU CAN USE TO ENJOY AN AUTOMATIC INCOME FOR LIFE

Surely, you've heard stories of the hard-driving executive who works twelve hours a day ... brings home a filled briefcase ... spends weekends doing paperwork ... ignores his family ... passes up vacations ... and gets $100,000 a year plus an early ulcer or heart attack for all his dedication. This is not our picture of success. A hundred thousand dollars a year is worthless if you can't enjoy the money.

You can avoid this trap of killing work—and still have the kin_ c. .noney normally associated with such an executive's life—*if* you understand the concept we like to call an "automatic income."

AN AUTOMATIC INCOME FOR LIFE IS POSSIBLE

What is an automatic income? As simply as possible, it means setting up your business affairs in such a fashion that you get an income without worry or work. You are the manager, the supervisor, the decision-maker, the main wheel that makes everything work. But, the day-to-day details of running the business are handled by people you hire, or who work for a "piece of the action." An automatic income will enable you to:

- Earn money without spending all your waking hours on the job;
- Travel for prolonged periods of time knowing that your business affairs are running smoothly;
- Devote time to hobbies, sports, or just plain relaxing;
- Provide everything you ever wanted for your family *without* neglecting them.

This is not an idle dream. If you've followed our suggestions during the previous chapters, you should understand by now that a lot of money can be earned by investments and business deals that virtually run themselves.

Here we will give you some hints to follow so you can lay your own foundation for an automatic income for life.

HOW TO GAIN YOUR OWN AUTOMATIC INCOME

Once you understand and believe that an automatic income is possible, half the battle is won. Strangely enough, this is a stumbling block to most wealth seekers. It is also the reason why many of them, even if they do become rich, seldom really enjoy their money. Here are the pointers:

- Every day, try to work less. This may seem strange, but is our way of demonstrating a fundamental principle. In other words—don't get so wrapped up in your business that you begin to feel that you're the only one who understands it and can run it properly. Instead, you should actively seek a way of delegating some of your day-to-day responsibilities to someone else. In the beginning, you will certainly have to do a lot of the work yourself, but, recognize this as a temporary situation, and don't let yourself be trapped in day-to-day details.
- Learn the secrets of the pyramid. No, we don't mean

you should take up some ancient Egyptian cult. Rather, you should actively seek ways to build one enterprise upon another until you have a truly impressive structure. For example: if you have one going business, you can easily get a loan to start another business; if your business permits, add new lines or related activities. If you've made some money selling real estate in the residential market, branch out to industrial real estate. You get the idea.

- Keep in mind that your fundamental goal is to make money with as little work and worry as possible. Don't get so interested in one business that you forget everything else. There is a great deal to be said for liking your work; but don't get so absorbed that you never look up to see other opportunities passing by.

- Cash in *at the right time.* What is the right time? That will vary with the business you're running, but certain clues are unmistakable. If the business stops growing as rapidly as you had hoped ... if your work load increases disproportionately to your profits ... if it seems your market potential has been reached ... these and other signs you will recognize yourself should tell you to look at the future carefully. It's tempting to hang on to a going business to see if it will bust out and grow; but, each year will only put you that much further from your goal of an automatic income.

If you follow these suggestions, you may find yourself in the position of Leo R. who had started a small, but profitable messenger service in a suburb of a big city. The business prospered and in time Leo had a good chunk of all the messenger businesses in the area going to the city. He especially built up this aspect of his messenger business by instituting regular trips to the city, whether or not he had any deliveries in the truck. This reputation soon got him in an enviable position; but, it also took a lot of work on Leo's part.

Leo worked hard. He even drove the truck himself if it seemed a driver would be late; his family saw too little of him. Then *it* happened. Those "slight pains" were cause for concern, said his doctor, and he put Leo in bed for nearly three months.

Then a strange thing happened. Leo's business continued almost unchanged. Loyal employees kept the place humming and you would never know that Leo wasn't at the helm. By the time Leo was mended enough to go back to work, he had come to a big decision. He virtually "gave away" his business to several key employees. All Leo wanted in return was a percentage of the profits for fifteen years in the future. This was truly an automatic income for Leo and amounted to over $100,000 during those fifteen years.

Leo found the secret of the automatic income and started several other businesses in years to come. And, after a few years, he was reaping between fifteen and twenty thousand dollars a year from the various businesses he started and "sold" to employees—each time increasing his annual automatic income.

CHECKLIST OF AUTOMATIC INCOME TECHNIQUES

Your success in achieving an automatic income will depend on how well you understand the various money-making techniques we have outlined for you. To re-cap, and make them firmly remembered:

- Borrowing is the secret of wealth today; understand the principle of Total Borrowing.
- Your first step is to build your credit reputation; the rest will then be easy.
- You can borrow more than money; learn where you can "borrow" time, talent and other non-cash items for your business needs.
- Always look for a situation that permits leverage; you'll multiply your money power several times over in such cases.
- Don't be afraid to ask; your friends, business associates, customers, creditors, and even your Government are all anxious to see you succeed. You will be surprised at the help you can get if you just ask.

Finally, the last item on our checklist is *you*. Look at yourself seriously as a wealth seeker now that you've come this far. We hope we've shown you that you need little beyond your ambition to become wealthy—everything else can be borrowed. We can't give you that drive to succeed. But, if you've read this far, we're pretty confident you're serious about making your own personal fortune.

Good luck!